Take Your Turn!

A Leadership Guide to Success for Young Women

Tonya L. Carter

TAKE YOUR TURN!
A Leadership Guide for Young Women

Tonya L. Carter
Gainesville, VA 20155
APearlPlusConsulting.com

In Association with:
Elite Online Publishing
63 East 11400 South
Suite #230
Sandy, UT 84070

EliteOnlinePublishing.com

ISBN # 978-1513676975 (Paperback)
ISBN # 979-8597101798 (Amazon Paperback)

HL.

FREE BONUS!

**Become one of Tonya's PEARLs so you can
"Take Your Turn" to lead or guide others to lead!
Visit www.aPearlPlusConsulting.com**

Your information will be kept private.

Foreword

Growing up in New York, I was not much of a reader – novels, history books, or any of the summer reading assignments. In fact, books like **"The Great Gatsby"** was simply a bore. I found no thrill, no common language, nor ability to relate to the story at all. But, like many school students in the 70's and 80's, you had no choice but to read what was assigned by English Teachers and approved by School Boards. What was missing, yet common throughout the US, is that almost every school required students to read books that were very much British, European, and early American.

Where were the black novels, where were the African American writers, and why aren't any of the characters in the books we were forced to read relatable? Sure, there were women authors, but many of their stories were based on experiences I would never encounter. I felt unable to delve into reading simply because I had no interest in trying to find familiarity in an unfamiliar world. It wasn't until I entered college, attending the first HBCU (Cheyney University), that I was introduced to books and novels that sparked my interest. Black and African America writers, Hispanic and Latino novelists, Native American and Asian authors that I had never known existed. Not to mention women authors who told me about me; and how to become a better me.

I currently have three unpublished manuscripts, not because I don't want to see them on the shelves, but because for me, writing was therapeutic. At some point, I will publish them, especially when I see the writings of phenomenal authors like Tonya Carter. She is absolutely someone I found to be not only intriguing, but completely relatable. An African America, female leader, passionate about her work and her writing. *"Take Your Turn: A Leadership Guide for Young Women"* has to be one of the best self-help and leadership writings I have read; and trust me, in my field, I've read several. Reading Tonya's manuscript gave me a perspective of what the younger generation of women leaders should aspire to become, and Tonya has written this guide to help prepare them for destiny.

I believe my favorite two chapters were *"Stronger Thank You Think"* and *"Keep Your Eyes On The Prize"*. When I read those chapters, I saw myself persevering to pursue my goals and dreams at an early age. Struggle for black girls is extremely hard, but when you are told to go against the grain and inspired to reach higher, you can accomplish anything. Combining positive reinforcement with an occasional athletic perspective is an added bonus. Therefore, both young men and young women can relate to these chapters, walking away with a stronger than you think mind-set and a laser focus on goals.

My other favorite chapter, *"Keep Your Eyes On The Prize"*, with emphasis on focus and positive attitude, is vitally important. How many times are we told "you can't" or "you won't be able to" or "why try, you'll only fail"? These are the beginning and ending of statements heard far too often for young black women. However, in the military, no matter which branch you are in, you are pushed to knowing your potential and focus on being strong. My father was an Army Sergeant and he made sure my two brothers, my sister and I knew that we were all equally capable of doing any and everything. Keeping your eye on the prize is not just a coined phrase, it is a way of life.

Today, I am the head of Talent Acquisition North America for a global company, I am the National President of the largest African American Human Resources organization, and a Women's Ministry leader. At the company I work for, I manage teams in the US, Canada and Latin America and member of the Center of Excellence global team. For my organization, I sit on a National Board and the

Office of the Chairman, with over 50 chapters under my leadership. And for my church, I have served in Ministry for over 30 years. Thus, Chapter 6 *"Stronger Than You Think"* and Chapter 10 *"Keep Your Eyes On The Prize"* resonated with me for all of the challenges that I have overcome as an African American woman.

Tonya represents women in leadership, not just in the essence of this guided message, but in her profession and life application. I trust that anyone who reads *"Take Your Turn: A Leadership Guide For Young Women"* will find nuggets of valuable advice, direction, and inspiration to reach beyond what seems unreachable. You will find yourself in one, if not many of the chapters and encouraged that you can do anything you put your mind to. While you are young, dare to dream and become the leader you were meant to be. Thank you, Tonya, for reaching back and paying it forward for young women who will soon lead!

Erika Broadwater
National President, Executive Board of Directors and Office of the Chairman National Association of African Americans in Human Resources

Table of Contents

Introduction

November 14, 2011 was just another day in traffic for me. For those of you who are familiar with the DC/Maryland/Virginia rush hour, you might be familiar with the experience, that two-hour traffic jam trek. Nothing was playing on the radio that I enjoyed, so I was left with my own thoughts. I was remembering a time when I was about 10 or 11 years old. I was a huge 'tom boy' who was willing to participate in anything that the guys were playing. I tended to be the only girl out there, but I was also often one of the first to be chosen for a team. One day, we were about to play football in the quad in front of our townhouses. While we were waiting for enough kids to come out to play, somehow we got on to the topic of what we wanted to be when we grew up. When it was my turn, I said:

- The first woman to play in the NBA for the Washington Bullets as a small forward (They laughed, but I wasn't kidding)

- An artist (because I really liked to sketch)

- An engineer (if the first two didn't work out)

One of the guys responded that I couldn't be an engineer because I'm a girl. An argument ensued. I don't remember much of what was said, but I remember how I felt . . . **ANGRY**! I made them pay by scoring a couple of touchdowns as a wide receiver, and no one got by me when I held the free safety position that day!

When I went inside after the game, I asked my mother if it was true that I couldn't be an engineer because I'm a girl, and her response was, "Baby, you can be whoever and whatever you want to be." My mom, my biggest cheerleader, continued to encourage me until I did become that engineer many years later. This situation may have created a proverbial "chip" on my shoulder. I've always been competitive, but something was triggered that day to fight to **TAKE MY TURN!**

Fast forward back to my car and I think how at least we now have networks and forums and clubs and societies that exist to encourage, guide, and mentor young women in choosing roles and careers that tend to be predominantly male. However, what struck me was that I wasn't aware of any foundational guidance offered to young women about choosing leadership roles or effectively leading others during the formative stage of making key life decisions. As the mother of two beautiful daughters – *yes I'm biased*! – I wondered if this could be a disadvantage for them as they considered their futures. When you look at the top leadership of most larger organizations, it's common to see very few women. While in high school, I don't remember leadership roles being encouraged for young women overall, unless it was to pad their resumes for college. As an example, I remember a suggestion from my Guidance Counselor to pursue the Secretary of the Spanish Club, not because it was meaningful, but more of a means to an end. Add to that, it was never the President or Vice President role that was recommended to me. It was more about participation in extracurricular activities versus leading them. Again, nothing meaningful. What I also remember is that young men were encouraged and groomed to lead from a very early age. Add to that the desire for young men to be the "alpha male," and the cultural norm that women are better suited for support roles. Which begs the following questions: 1. How does a young woman compete when she wants her turn to lead? 2. Are the issues the same for young women today as it was for me and the generations before mine? 3. Whatever the potential roadblocks, how can young women prepare to become successful future leaders?

Using a story-telling style, mixed with other shared perspectives and some evidentiary support, this book is meant to help answer these questions for and help to equip young women at a time in their lives when they can prepare to be effective leaders in the future. Note that the examples will be from men and women because that is the world we live in, and we need to be comfortable with how to work together effectively. However, it also serves another purpose; to provide tools for adult leaders, parents, guardians, and mentors to invest in those young women. The evidentiary support is primarily for the adult facilitators, so don't feel bad if that informational part doesn't resonate with you as the reader. A Leader Facilitation Guide is also available separately to offer facilitators a continuous learning approach for each chapter, to which they can use the included activities and/ or add their own exercises.

If you are seeking self-improvement as the reader, you can complete the activities at the end of each chapter in private. However, for growth purposes, I recommend identifying someone you trust to check-in with, run your ideas by, or gauge if they see a difference in your leadership skills, and to plan the next practice steps.

My hope is that this book might help change the landscape of top leaders to be more representative of the female population. This book is not meant to be a rigid set of rules or a checklist, but rather to offer guidelines and different perspectives so that readers are able to create their own paths for their personal leadership journeys.

Keep in mind that no exact formula for success exists. Each individual journey might seem similar, but it is actually different. Hopefully, this book will help readers ask the right questions so that they feel more confident about their personal journeys, or they will be enabled to better give guidance to their daughters, nieces, granddaughters, students, protégés, etc.

Young males may also find this book helpful; however, this is written based on the unique set of issues some women face when they pursue leadership roles in a culture that is predominantly male dominated. The premise is that it will offer tips, real life and relevant examples, and encouragement to teen women aged 13 – 18 on how to effectively prepare to lead others, specifically focusing on the trend of topics that were expressed in the survey results (details below).

Data Analysis:

When I initially began to gather data on this topic, I conducted several interviews with students in April 2010, I was coaching high school track and field along with my day job. My youngest daughter and son had made the team, so as usual, I threw myself into being involved with this part of their lives. It also allowed me a unique advantage to observe up close and personal some of the subject matter. I also used Facebook to pick the brains of a few hundred other young women in high school or who recently had started to attend college with the following question:

What concern(s) have you had, or do you have about pursuing leadership roles from a female's perspective?

The following were the responses I received from most to least frequent:

- fear of not being taken seriously (most frequent)

- fear of failure (lack of confidence)

- fear of rejection

- fear of criticism

- fear of having to lead strong personalities (fear of conflict)

- fear of leading peers

- fear of stereotypes

- fear of being a "token" leader

The results bothered me, but I couldn't initially put my finger on why. Was it that I was disappointed because I personally took a fearless approach to living my life, or was it something else?

Then life got in the way, and I set this endeavor aside for ten years. However, my interest was sparked again with discussions within our society on the news, talk shows, conferences, social media, etc. about the Equal Rights Amendment. Advocates from the WNBA, women's professional soccer leagues, and other professional athletes started coming forward to publicly put a voice to the inequities they saw between significant pay differentials between men and women for the same roles. In some cases, some of the women's events were even more well attended. Then women politicians continued to be a rising topic. Did you know that when women run for elected office in the United States, they win at the same rates as men? But women, on average, have to be asked by community leaders more often before they'll launch a serious candidacy. According to the American University School of Public Affair's Women and Politics Institute, women make up only 24 percent of state legislatures, 17 percent of Congress, 8 percent of the 100 largest city's mayors, and 12 percent of state governors when they are the majority of voters, and make up half of the population in the US (www.sheshouldrun.org). All these issues popping up reignited my passion for this subject. And, finally, on a more personal note, several of my friends and peers had finished writing books that they felt led to write despite their own busy family lives and careers. There wasn't any reason for me to not start again.

So, I pulled out my notes and having gained ten more years of experience as an HR professional,

I realized why my previous summary of findings bothered me. I had asked a leading question! The way I asked the question led the respondents to answer negatively. This doesn't mean that negative things don't happen on our leadership journey, but it's not all that happens. The best way to help equip others for their journey is to offer a balanced perspective using a positive approach.

Instead of one leading interview question, I created a survey through SurveyMonkey, and sent the shareable link with instructions to previous participants, my network of classmates, work colleagues, high schools around the continental US, my Sorority Chapter members, my military network, my friends, my children and their friends, and others (@619 invitations). This approach offered me more opportunity to slice the data in numerous ways: generationally, regionally, challenges faced (or not), etc. The average time to complete the survey was less than 6 minutes. There were 190 respondents for a response rate of slightly over 30%, making the analyzed data valid. The survey questions consisted of the following:

1. Keeping in mind that there is overlap in the timeline as well as personal values for Generations, what Generation do you identify with most?

    a. Traditionalists – Core Values: Adhere to rules, Conformity is good, Loyalty, and Trust in government. Education is a dream. (1922 – 1943)

b. Baby Boomers – Core Values: Anti-war & government, Equal Rights & opportunity, Radicals, and "Live to Work". Education is a birthright. (1944 – 1964)

c. Generation X – Core Values: Global thinking, Cautious with money, Flexibility, "Work to Live" for work/life balance. Education is expected. (1965 – 1980)

d. Generation Y/Millennials – Core Values: Ambitious, Individuality, Want meaningful work, Tolerant, and Accepts differences. Education is debt. (1981 – 2000)

e. Generation Z – Core Values: Diversity, Actions speak louder than words, Social Media, Altruistic, and Influencers. Education comes in many forms. (2001 – Present)

2. What region in the US did you attend intermediate, middle, and high school?

a. North

b. South

c. East Coast

d. West Coast

e. Mid-West

f. Central

g. Multiple regions

h. Other

Comments to explain g or h response:

_____

_____

_____

3. Which trait do you identify with most?

a. Introvert – Tend to enjoy more time to themselves, are very aware of their internal thoughts and recharge more in solitude.

b. Extravert – Are often more outspoken, outgoing, and absolutely love being around other people, gaining energy from their surroundings.

c. Ambivert – Have a blend of traits from both introverts and extroverts, as well as their own unique strengths.

4. Do you/Did you have a desire to lead between the ages of 13 and 18?

   a. Yes

   b. No

Comments to explain:

_____

_____

_____

5. Do you have or have you had an encourager/coach who's been a constant presence in your life?

   c. Yes

   d. No

Comments:

_____

_____

_____

6. Do you have or did you have a general idea/direction of your interests between 13 and 18?

   a. Yes

   b. No

Comments to explain if it has remained the same or not:

_____

_____

_____

7. What was/is, if any, the top challenge you faced pertaining to leadership opportunities between 13 and 18?

   a. Gender

   b. Culture

   c. Stereotypes

   d. Lack of opportunity

   e. Single Parent Household (to include geographically)

   f. No challenges/barriers

   g. Other

Comments to explain, with specific examples:

_____

_____

_____

8. If any, how did you overcome the challenges you identified in the previous
   question?

Comments to explain, with specific examples:

_____

_____

_____

9. What else would you like to share about
   your leadership journey that may help
   others?

Comments:

_____

_____

_____

10. Contact Information (OPTIONAL) -
    Privacy Statement: Your contact infor-
    mation will be kept confidential, and
    not be shared with others without your
    expressed consent, or that of your par-
    ent or guardian if you are a minor. Your
    contact information will only be used to
    follow up for clarification of content that
    you shared in the survey, or request to
    use the content that you shared in the

survey within the book, and acknowledge you for it.

Name

Email Address

Phone Number

The trending responses are what customized the topics covered in each chapter. This book is tailored specifically to these with a few topics thrown in for what I wish I'd learned when I was 13. The last question offered the opportunity to follow up with survey takers who shared compelling comments which might lead to stories that could be helpful to others on their leadership journey.

Let's look at a summary of the data analysis. Lori Hess Tompos is also a leader in Training & Development with her own business, Avail Consulting. She is also my classmate and friend. I wanted a third party to summarize the data from the survey to prevent unconsciously making conclusions that I wanted. So, she volunteered to delve into the details of the results of the survey and engaged her daughter Laurel to analyze the statistics and summarizes the information below.

As seen by the survey questions noted in this Introduction, we looked at leadership interest, aspirations, and barriers by generation, region, and personality. The survey was shared with approximately 619 women, of which 190 responded. That is a response rate of over 30%. Of the sample size, Traditionalists made up 4% of the responses, 14% were Baby Boomers, 38% Gen X, 30% GenY, and 14% Gen Z.

Of this sample size, regional data identified that just over 56% of the entire group attended high school (grades 9 – 12) on the East Coast (34%) or in the Mid-West (22%). Rounding out the sample group was the South at 17%, the West Coast at 14%, and the North at 9%. Women raised in multiple regions made up the final 4%.

From a personality perspective, over 52% of the group considered themselves to be "Ambiverts", meaning that they prefer a blend of traits from both Extraverts (22%) and Introverts (26%). Technically, someone who identifies themselves as an Ambivert desires time together with friends and family, as well as time to be alone and recharge their "batteries". It's helpful to have an awareness about what gives you energy and what activities refresh you because then you can optimize your time to give your best effort, be your best self, and honor your preferences.

What was surprising is that many of this sample had a strong desire to lead at this age. Although Traditionalists had the smallest sample size, they had the highest affirmative response rate at 100%. However, the desire to lead remained consistently strong across each generation for an affirmative response of 61% across all of them, no matter what region they went to school or their personality type.

It was good to see that the majority did have the support of a Coach, Mentor, or Supporter at 62%. Many of them cited their parents as their main supporters and "Encouragers". Not having someone to fill the support role was identified as being a "Lack of Opportunity" barrier. But, it was especially good to see that the current generation, Gen Z, affirmed that 80% of them had someone to fill this role in their lives.

Another surprise was that overall, 70% of the women knew the general direction of their career interests were between 13-18 years of age, whether in a broad sense (e.g. "I'd like to work with children.") or more specifically (e.g. "I'd like to be a veterinarian.") Gen X and Gen Y had a response rate of over 75%, while Gen Z's positive response rate of "Yes" was closer to 85%, indicating that young ladies are becoming more aware of their career interests, as shown by the trending increase over the last three generations.

In this sample group, Baby Boomers experienced the most barriers at 88%, the biggest categories being Stereotypes and Culture that were not supportive of women as leaders. As one Baby Boomer reflected, "Men were programmed to lead.

Women were not. Women were told that while they could be 'second', they could not be first." The percentage of women with perceived barriers to leadership is 68% overall, Gen X had 66%, Gen Y 65%, and Gen Z 62%. However, again we see a positive trend with decreasing perceived barriers from generation to generation.

Although the percentage of barriers seems to be decreasing, there is still an overall common theme to the barriers experienced after the Baby Boomers. Traditionalists and Baby Boomers claim that stereotypes and cultural issues were the primary roadblocks for them, but Lack of Opportunity was either the first or second barrier for the remaining three generations. Those who listed "Other", when explained actually fell under "Lack of Opportunity" (e.g. Lack of accessibility, finances, resources, or services).

With a smaller sample size, we're not able to make any definitive conclusions, but the trend of the data indicates that 13 – 18 is the right time to practice leadership skills for tentative plans for the future, and that Gen Z is ripe for the knowledge shared in this book. Trends of the increased support decrease of perceived barriers, overall desire to lead, and basic understanding of their career interests opens a world of possibilities for them.

As you start your leadership journey to prepare to **Take Your Turn**, I leave you with this quote from

John C. Maxwell, an American author, speaker, and pastor whose work has primarily focused on leadership. "Dreams don't work unless you do." Congratulations on choosing to act toward your future as a leader!

CHAPTER 1

A Leadership Perspective

lead·er·ship
/ˈlēdərˌSHip/

is the art of motivating a group of people
to act toward achieving a common goal.
Although identified as a noun, in my opinion,
effective leadership requires action,
indicating that it is more of a verb.

Starting with a clear leadership perspective is important to the foundation for readers to build upon. One survey taker shared that, *"Establishing leadership roles as a child/teen is vital and I encourage parents/guardians to find opportunities for their children to lead in school/their community."* and another, Alaisha A., noted that, *"The leadership positions I held between the ages of 13-18 helped prepare for leadership responsibilities in the military and as an educator."* I see 13 - 18 years of age as being the formative years for establishing that foundation to become a successful leader. So why isn't there more information and guidance available to aid with preparing and equipping them to do so? I couldn't be the only one to feel this way, could I? When I decided to write this book, it became noticeably clear that I was not the only one to think so. I was met with resounding support that the approach I was taking was needed. I hope to provide an initial toolkit that will equip aspiring leaders and those who coach or mentor them and make my supporters proud with the final results.

So, I had a very engaging conversation with a friend and West Point alum of mine, Matthew S. His wife, Kim, is one of my best friends, and she suggested that he call to seek my advice as a professional HR leader, and we ended up also reminiscing about our time as officers in the Army. I had shared a story about my strong desire to lead my soldiers during Desert Storm. I knew my role was to bring everyone home safely, but also discovered that they felt the same about me. They wanted to protect me as much as I wanted to protect them. It concerned me because I was a woman leading an all-male vertical construction Corps of Engineers Platoon. Was this because of an innate feeling of the men to protect the women, or just being a cohesive unit? Matt then shared the following: "*We've been told all of our lives that there are two types of people in the world; wolves and the sheep they prey upon. That's not really true. There's a third type, and they serve as the shepherds that protect the sheep from the wolves. Words such as 'Duty', 'Faith', and 'Honor' ring true for them and they desire to be associated with others like them. The heroes that run into burning buildings, defend their country, and patrol our highways are shepherds. The 20-year-old soldier who lays down her life in a faraway place protecting her squad is a shepherd. We celebrate them because they are the ones who keep the wolves at bay.*"

These profound words resonated with me, and I realized that I may have contributed to my soldiers' response to protect me by modeling shepherd-like behavior in wanting to protect them. Each of us would have laid down our lives for the other while we protected our country, or whatever country we were protecting at the time, creating the mindset of a cohesive unit. As individuals, we knew how to do our jobs well, but together we were exceptional.

Most leaders won't need to deal with life or death decisions, but this may help put things into perspective. You will read more about the styles of leadership, but here is a glimpse of leadership in action, serving and supporting others to achieve success, and ultimately help a company/ organization thrive. Did you even realize that you can lead and serve at the same time? But I get ahead of myself.

As Lori assisted with interviewing some of the survey takers who offered some intriguing comments about leadership, she also shared some of her own thoughts on leadership that are captured below:

I often get asked the question, "Are leaders born or made?" I always say, "Yes". Leaders are born and maybe you may have been granted some gifts in terms of leadership abilities, but you want to cultivate them that so you are the best leader that you can be. Take your talent, your strengths, and your unique aptitudes, and do all that you can with it. Be a leader for greater good and with purpose. You must actually care about the people in your group, treat them always with respect, and genuinely be concerned with their welfare. You must develop relationships and trust in those bonds. You must always work ethically and morally. You need to be a good listener and you have to be a good motivator. You have to have vision, purpose, meaning, and direction in everything that you do, and you must have passion around those goals. You have to identify and honor your values and you have to live in alignment with your values, your strengths, and your virtues.

This is a tall order, by design. "Anything worth doing is worth doing well," as the saying goes. Thus, if you do not want to be the leader, no problem. Then, be the best follower and the best support person possible. Regardless of your role, be the best team member you can be.

There are several types of leadership styles. All of them serve a purpose and can lead to success. As a firm believer and certified trainer in the Situational Leadership concept offered by Ken Blanchard, it is helpful to understand each, and engage in that style when needed, even if you are naturally stronger at one over another. Ken Blanchard focuses on four primary leadership styles: Directing, Coaching, Supporting, and Delegating. The choice for which leadership style to use is based on correctly diagnosing the developmental stage of the person or people to be led from their demonstrated behavioral characteristics (*Situational Leadership II*, Ken Blanchard Group, 2020). Each of these four leadership styles are captured within the following list of leadership styles below. Keep in mind that this is not an all-inclusive list of leadership styles, and some may be referred to by other names, but are the ones noted most often in my studies of adult learning.

- Democratic/Participative Leadership Style
- Autocratic Leadership Style
- Transformational Leadership Style
- Transactional Leadership Style
- Laissez Faire Leadership Style

The democratic or participative leadership style is leadership that is based on "power with" rather than "power over" others. It focuses on facilitating a democratic process that empowers others. The best description that I found of this style and that I believe will be recognized by this target audience is in Democratic Principals in Action: Eight Pioneers written by Joseph Blase and others in 1995. This style would work well with Principals and teachers at a school. Leading by consensus offers a very collaborative approach but can make the decision process a bit lengthy. Keeping this in mind when decisions require a quick turnaround will be important when using this leadership style.

The autocratic leadership style is more authoritative in nature. These leaders often make decisions with little or no input from others. They have a very clear vision of what they want to happen, and when and where it should happen. This would work very well in launching a new business scenario but would have the opposite effect when working with long standing and experienced subject matter experts. The latter would see this leadership style as micromanagement.

Transformational leadership is about inspiring positive change. Leaders who use this style are not only deeply involved in the process for making change, but also focused on ensuring that every member of the team is successful for their contribution. You often see this leadership style tied with specific projects for which the leader is passionate. Studies by Alice H. Eagly, Mary C. Johannesen, and Marloes L. van Engen (Psychological Bulletin, Vol 129(4), Jul 2003, 569-591) in 2003 found that female leaders were more transformational than male leaders, and that this is one of the more effective leadership styles. I equate this one to being a Servant Leader as described in the opening of this chapter.

With the next style, S. P. Robbins defines transactional leadership as when "Leaders who lead primarily by using social exchanges for transactions" (Robbins, 2007, p.475). Basically, a reward system is in place to acknowledge successful completion of performance tasks. As the title says, it is very transactional in nature. For instance, this would be the case if a manager provides a bonus to an employee for accomplishing a professional certification needed for achieving the team's vision, or for a student getting bonus points for extra credit. The same studies for transformational leadership noted in the previous paragraph indicates that female leaders are more likely to engage in a reward approach for meeting expectations than male leaders.

Finally, laissez-faire leadership is known as a delegative leadership style. It is where the leader tends to be more "hands-off" allowing the team members to make their own decisions. Leaders need to be careful here because productivity can be impacted negatively if the team members are not capable of conducting the work delegated to them. This leadership style is best suited for a long standing, experienced team of people who are deemed as subject matter experts in their fields/industries.

As a certified facilitator of Situational Leadership II under the Ken Blanchard program, one exercise that I've conducted many times over the last 10+ years during the Situational Leadership workshops is called the Match/Mis-match exercise, which clearly demonstrated the connection/disconnection within a controlled setting. The idea was to get a sense of what it feels like to try to match a certain leadership style with the development level of the team member through a role play activity. The acting leaders and employees have a scenario and must stay within their assigned character. The two most noticeable gaps occurred when the leader used a directive or autocratic style of leadership with a team member who had the expertise to run with a basic vision of what needed to be accomplished. We consistently saw the same disconnect with leaders trying to delegate to those team members who needed more direction, as they were relatively new to the role.

I share this because I am a strong supporter of matching your leadership style with that of the developing team member. Although the team members own their development, in order for a leader to be effective, it is important for the leader to invest in the growth and development of the individual team members and the team as a whole in order to achieve the overall vision for what they are responsible for. If you don't, it would be like driving a car with one or more flat tires.

To accomplish this, there is no one tool that will do it. You need to maintain a toolkit full of options because it's important to meet the team member where they're at and help them to achieve their highest potential. Diagnosing where they are, then matching them with the appropriate leadership styles is more likely to assist in their development and create a stronger relationship with them because of your investment. It's a very fluid process and breeds trust and loyalty, resulting in retaining a cohesive, well-equipped team. In my opinion and personal experience, this developmental mindset is what makes the difference in helping to make teams and organizations more effective.

This is exactly why I choose not to label any of the leadership styles as bad, or better than the others. There is a time and purpose for each. It's important for us as leaders to recognize the proper time to use each one effectively. The leadership style needed may not be your strong suit, but that's why you surround yourself with team members who can strengthen those areas as you genuinely develop and invest in them.

Consequently, sometimes, even when we are in the lead role, it may be best to follow. What I mean by this is that strong leaders recognize and admit when they are not the strongest in a particular area and are willing to move out of the way for someone else to step for the likelihood of a positive outcome. Leaders don't always need to lead from the front. It's what is known as followership.

foll·ow·er·ship
/fol'oh ər ship/

is the capacity or willingness to follow others

Have you ever noticed informal leaders within a group and how they influence others? They don't have an official title, but clearly the group trusts the individual enough to take their advice. Those individuals wouldn't get the opportunity if the leader by title didn't step aside to some extent. There is a level of humility that the actual leader needs to portray. Leaders don't know everything and should be willing to say so. When that occurs, and you encourage others to step up to lead and share their expertise, the possibilities for growth are high. You learn. They practice. You build future leaders.

This is my high-level perspective on leadership, but I'd like to share another's insight that offers assistance on a way to start. Dr. Roy Alston, Ph.D., who retired as a Major from the Dallas Police Department, was a former Army Officer, and is a classmate and friend of mine. He clearly has the credentials to speak to leadership. It is my intent here to share another perspective because it gives the readers an opportunity to form their own opinions and apply them in a way that makes the most sense for their leadership journey. Consider his offered and sage advice below as you begin to practice for yours. Roy . . .

I have had the opportunity to lead in many organizations. Along the way, I have learned that individuals who take the time to approach their entry into a new organization as a leader do far better when they take the time to be strategic in their approach. Some years ago, I came across the book, The First 90 Days: Critical Success Strategies for New Leaders at All Levels by Michael Watkins. The First 90 Days is about offering a way to make a smooth transition into a new leadership role and the timeline to be productive and add value to the organization. Each chapter of the book focuses on one of ten key transition strategies. The following is the three phased approach that I developed for myself when starting new leadership roles.:

Phase 1 -The First 30 Days; STOP to LISTEN and LEARN

The first phase is one of observation. Resist the urge to "fix things" immediately. The single biggest mistake new leaders make is trying to fix processes without truly understanding the what, why and how of it. Don't try to do too much. This will be difficult to do because your nature may be to try to contribute to show your worth. Instead, listen carefully rather than talk. Gather available information and ask questions. Find out who the "go to" people are and connect with them. Get to know the team on a personal level. The key lesson here is that to build relationships, they need to know that you genuinely care about them.

Share your personal leadership philosophy with the team: how you plan to lead, your core values, your expectations and what others can expect of you, what you won't tolerate, your pet-peeves and that you're open to feedback as you are learning and growing in this new role.

Phase 2 – The Second 30 Days; MOVE SLOWLY to CLARIFY

Take time to understand the communication styles within your team. Who prefers details? Who wants just the highlights? Who needs to hear a message more than once before they really understand? Your communication style may be different than theirs, but you can model their style to clearly get your point across. This is extremely important because failure to effectively communicate in a way that others can understand you will make it difficult to succeed as a leader.

Take your time to ensure that you have a strong sense of the team members' communication styles. Spend time asking questions so that you can clarify whether you've read the style accurately.

Phase 3 – The Third 30 Days; GO to ALIGN and COMMUNICATE

In the final phase, clearly communicate the expectations. Expectations may already exist. Just confirm that they are clear and correct before holding the team accountable to them. Modify them as needed based on any new information that is communicated to you from a higher level of leadership. If your efforts and communication are aligned with their vision, the more likely you will succeed.

Always remember - navigating the transition period in a new leader role can feel a bit uncomfortable. This is normal. Team dynamics can be difficult to navigate. But if you take the time to find how you best fit within the team, and focus on building strong relationships, you'll be off to a great start and you will find the resources and help you need to be successful.

I have learned these things over the years and have coached others through the same process successfully. The process isn't perfect, but at least offers a plan for which you have control and can influence.

The First 90 Days is a helpful resource for starting any leadership journey or transitioning to a new leadership role. I'm pleased that Dr. Alston was able to share this leadership perspective. I would also keep in mind that 90-days is relative. The nature of the role may dictate whether you should spend less or longer than 90-days getting oriented and acclimated to your new surroundings.

I personally was able to watch this process in action when coaching the specialty events at my children's high school in 2012 for the girls' high school Indoor/Outdoor Track & Field. A young lady was chosen as one of the Team Captains. She spent the first couple of weeks observing what the Coach's requirements were and learning how to implement them when he wasn't around (e.g. warm-ups, stretching, cool downs, putting equipment way, etc.). Over the next few weeks she made sure to check in and clarify with the Coach that the communications she gave to the athletes were in alignment with his expectations, and continued to practice and build confidence in her ability to successfully complete the role. Finally, she was able to share communications and activities that were aligned with the Coach's expectations and vision without seeking his guidance each time or deviating from his plans, and became instrumental with before and after practice efforts, relieving some of the workload on the Coach. Not only did she grow in this leadership role, but her confidence in herself did too! That is a key purpose of this book; to help identify more opportunities like this for other young ladies to practice leadership during these formative years.

Now let's look at the first set of activities. The intent with the activities is to learn, apply, retain, and grow from the knowledge gained in each chapter. As mentioned in the introduction, if you choose for the activities to initially be done in private for self-paced improvement, I still recommend identifying a partner or mentor to gauge how things are going and decide on next steps once complete.

#TAKINGTHELEAD

ACTIVITY PAGE

What is your preferred leadership style? What is your secondary preference?

_____

_____

Why do you believe that these are your preferred leadership styles? Give specific examples tied back to the style description.

_____

_____

_____

_____

_____

_____

_____

_____

_____

_____

_____

_____

_____

_____

_____

APPLICATION

As you embark on a new role, follow the first 90 days model, and journal how it went.

_____

_____

_____

_____

_____

_____

_____

_____

_____

_____

_____

_____

_____

_____

_____

_____

_____

_____

_____

_____

_____

_____

_____

_____

TAKE YOUR TURN

CHAPTER 2

A Diamond in the Rough (Value)

val·ue
/ˈvalyo͞o/

is the worth, usefulness and importance of
someone

Eleanor Roosevelt, Former First Lady of the United States, once said, "No one can make you feel inferior without your consent." Don't consent. Ever. The preservation of your self-esteem is worth protecting. Listen to constructive guidance from people you trust and have built a positive relationship, but don't allow others to tear you down, to include yourself. **You are worth the investment!**

Ultimately, everyone has value. Some have just not been encouraged to see it in themselves. Our backgrounds may be different with some being tougher than others, but we all bring something unique to the table. We each have something worthwhile to share with others or contribute to a discussion or business. We each can be useful by lending a helping hand. Best of all, this means that you are important in the scheme of things! Don't let anyone steal that belief from you. Even if you do not hear these affirmations from others often, repeat them to yourself. Own them because **YOU ARE VALUABLE!** Claim your Crown! You are not here by accident! Each person is unique and has a special purpose in life. Find your top talents, your passions, and share them with the world.

I know that this is not always easy, but maybe this will help:

I along with many others going through puberty, struggled with my self-image. First I was too skinny. Then I was too fat. My glasses might as well have been coke bottles. Why didn't I have more friends like my sister, Angie. Everyone can list things about themselves that they don't like or wish they had so and so's . . . you fill in the blank. But how often do you give yourself a break? Have you ever considered that someone might wish that they had one of your attributes?

I learned early on how to cope with what I lack by focusing on what I do well. I didn't initially recognize that others complimented and encouraged me on the things that I did well because I was so caught up in what I was lacking. Sound familiar? Here's what happened when I started to understand how the encouragement tied to my strengths.

I realized that my mother and others thought that I was smart. Not only did they say it frequently, but I noticed that the gifts that I received for birthdays and Christmas were more academic in nature to support what they were saying. My dad would show off with his buddies by picking a word out of the dictionary or a magazine and say, "Watch this! Tonya, spell *electroencephalograph*." And I would. I was 8 or 9 at the time. His buddies were shocked and amazed, and you could see the pride on my dad's face.

Also, my parents and others often voiced how athletic I was. I was allowed to participate in many sports, to include playing with the guys because I could hold my own. My parents attended almost all my local competitions, cheered me on through some of the tougher ones, and expressed belief in me that I could beat a competitor the next time if I didn't at that time.

My mom was my loudest supporter. I could pick her voice out of the bleachers when they were packed, and it would pump me up. My dad would stand away from the crowd in a space relatively empty of others and use his calm coaching voice to help me focus on the fundamentals of what I needed to do. To this day, when I need encouragement, their voices are the ones I hear in my head pushing me to achieve more; be more. My affirmations: "There's nothing you can't do!" "You're more than enough!"

So, if you have difficulty identifying what you do well, ask someone who knows you. You may be a great friend or sibling, a good listener, a great dancer or speaker or writer. You may be great with animals, or you may know how to style hair without taking one lesson. Maybe you are extremely creative, or great with kids. Who knows, but there will always be something positive that you can note about yourself, and I bet you won't have to look awfully hard to find it.

One of the survey takers expressed that, *"It's important as a woman to know who you are, and your value and I wish I would have understood that at 13."* My experiences and some stories that I've captured are meant to help form and/or strengthen value and self-worth in each reader. Lisa W. nailed it when she shared, your *"opinion matters and . . . makes a difference. Everyone's voice matters. . . what you say and do makes a difference, and . . . you are a positive force."* Or, at least you can be if you recognize that you have value and self-worth.

Here's another real-life example that may inspire you. At one of my high school reunions, I spoke to a woman with whom I went to middle and high school. I told her, "I don't know if I ever told you this, but I admired you throughout middle and high school. To be honest, I wished I were you. You were the tall, beautiful (and she still is), cheerleader, put-together person that I wished I could be. You even made braces look good!" Then she shared an honest reflection of herself during that time of her life, and it made me realize that even when it looks like we have the perfect life to others, we all struggle with something. Here's Hillary N.'s story.

When I was 5 years old, I'd look out the window and feel sad, but I didn't understand why. I felt like everyone around me was living their lives, but I wasn't. As I grew older, for years my self-esteem and confidence were low, and I struggled with my self-worth. I would tremble and sweat all the time from being so nervous. I felt uncomfortable in my own skin. I was too tall, and too skinny. My mother encouraged me, but she also struggled with anxiety issues. As I got older, I felt the need to be validated. I never did anything alone. I pretended to be the person I wanted to be. What got me through is my strong family unit. They were supportive, and I never wanted to disappoint my parents. Art and fashion became a focus and outlet for me.

I was later diagnosed with clinical depression and social anxiety. At a low point in my life, while getting help, I was introduced to a book titled The Power of Now by Eckhart Tolle. It made me more self-aware and focus on now instead of worrying about the future. I regret that I "found" myself in my late 40's/early 50's, and not at an earlier age."

So as Nancy B. comments in the survey, *"Know your own self-worth! Create your own path."* Trust and believe that you can despite your circumstances, and don't wait to explore it. Time passes more quickly than you think.

Another surprising example of building value and self-worth came from a movie that I watched (several times). If you've never seen the movie The Help, I highly recommend it. This movie is a period film depicting America in the 1960's. It was released in 2011 and is based on Kathryn Stockett's 2009 book with the same title. There is one part of this movie that touches my heart every time I see it. Aibileen Clark, who is the main character, is an African American maid in Mississippi. She works for a socialite, Elizabeth Leefolt and cares for the Leefolts' daughter, Mae Mobley, whom Elizabeth is neglecting. Aibileen often tells Mae, "You is kind! You is smart! You is important!" You can see how these regular affirmations encourage Mae over time in the movie. My mother then started to repeat these affirmations to others; mostly children (at church, in her neighborhood, to her grandchildren), but even to me and my siblings, who were already adults by this time. What I found surprising was our response to hearing her repeat this quote to us.

Initially, we all thought it was cute, maybe even a little silly. We are adults, so what else could she do to encourage our self-esteem. She and Dad had raised us well. However, the more she said it, the more we internalized it and looked forward to her saying it again. You could see the pride in children's faces when my mother would say this to them. Without realizing it, me, my brother, and sisters did too.

So, build yourself and others up. Words have the power to help or hurt. Just as I started this chapter, I'll end it the same. The preservation of your self-esteem is worth protecting. Don't consent to allow others to take it from you, and I'll add to make every effort not to take it from others.

I hope that these stories help you realize that **you have value** and that **you are worthy!** You may just need to take a moment to affirm them. Here are some activities to help you practice.

#PRICELESS

ACTIVITY PAGE

List five things that you like about yourself.

_____

_____

_____

_____

_____

_____

_____

_____

What is the area(s) that you need affirmations in your life? Create affirmations for those areas that are clear and concise? (As an example, mine were "There's nothing you can't do!" "You're more than enough!")

_____

_____

_____

_____

_____

_____

_____

_____

_____

APPLICATION

For one week, when getting ready in the morning, look directly at your reflection in the mirror and repeat your affirmations to yourself aloud. If that makes you uncomfortable, note them on sticky notes, place them on the mirror, and read them to yourself. Note how you feel on the first day that you do this. At the end of the week, note how you feel. Repeat over time with new affirmations that come to light as you learn more about yourself.

_____

_____

_____

_____

_____

_____

_____

_____

_____

_____

_____

_____

_____

_____

_____

CHAPTER 3

You Be You
(Self Discovery)

au·then·tic·i·ty
/ˌôTHenˈtisədē/

genuinely staying true to yourself

D. H. Lawrence, an English writer and poet, said, "You've got to know yourself so that you can at last be yourself." Warren Bennis, an American scholar and author offers that, "Successful leadership is not about being tough or soft, sensitive or assertive, but about a set of attributes. First and foremost is character." These two quotes speak to knowing and growing yourself. After recognizing that you are valuable, which was addressed in the previous chapter, it's especially important to understand who you are and what you stand for so that you can live life as your best self. This chapter helps to offer information on your journey to self-discovery.

One survey taker's comment really resonated with me on this topic. Le'Ann F. stated, *"The key is to believe in yourself the most. You cannot let others determine who you are and what you are capable of. A good leader knows themselves, . . .".* This is so true, but we also must recognize that we evolve as we learn more about ourselves. Maegen G. expressed, *"You mold your identity along the way. It consistently changes and evolves."* As you grow in your self-discovery, this is the case.

I am an avid fan of Carla Harris, the first female African American Vice President on Wall Street! My husband introduced me to her on YouTube several years ago, and I was hooked. After having read her books, and watching her videos on YouTube, I had the opportunity to hear her speak at a Women's Conference in Austin, Texas in 2019. She was just as mesmerizing in person as she was on YouTube, only better because I got a signed book from her through my colleague Mindy! But I digress.

At the conference Carla shared her Pearls of Wisdom for being a successful leader, and one of them is authenticity. She says that *"This is at the heart of your power. Your authenticity is your distinct competitive advantage; no one can be you like you can . . . Most people are not comfortable in their own skin, so when they see someone who is, they gravitate to that person. Bring your authentic self to the table and people will trust you."* The part where she says, *". . . no one can be you like you can . . ."* catches my attention each time I hear her say it or re-read it in <u>Expect to Win</u> on the very first page. It speaks to how unique we are as individuals; that we have something special to share. There really is only one you.

It brings to mind how often I worked hard to act like my male counterparts or leaders because I thought that to get ahead I needed to model them in this predominantly male environment of Engineering. I found myself walking and talking like them. Initially, it wasn't too difficult because I grew up a bit of a tomboy. However, as I matured, it made me feel uncomfortable in my own skin. It was hard to sustain this faux Tonya.

But one day, something happened that gave me a glimpse of my authentic self, and I liked what I saw. I was a young leader in the Army. During a military exercise, I and other young leaders were given an assignment. The scenario described the military situation that we were walking into. I had not been at my best in the initial stages of the exercise. I was nervous and trying to act like someone I wasn't. I'd listen and try to explain perspectives that were not my own, and you can guess how well that went. Since I felt like I was failing, I took a step back, and studied the scenario more closely, and picked up on a couple of things:

1. The enemy was attacking us in what appeared to be a random pattern, and there didn't seem to be a clear purpose.

2. Our troops responded with a small force each time that they did this.

So, I thought back on my military studies, and remembered that the US style of interaction tends to be reactive, so when I looked at the big picture of the battlefield, I realized that these random attacks had one thing in common. They consistently occurred away from the most likely approach for a larger enemy force to come through. EUREKA! These were diversionary tactics!

So, when we had to present to a visiting General the next day, although nervous, I was able to share my findings for my portion with a level of calm conviction. It made sense to my perspective, not because I was repeating what others told me to say. I used a laser pointer and would smoothly circle the areas of concern with the light so that they wouldn't see my hands shaking. When I had completed my presentation, I was met with total silence. Crickets could literally be heard since we were in the field. Inside I was disappointed because I thought I must have missed the mark . . . again, but I schooled my facial features so that they wouldn't know the turmoil that I was feeling. I squeezed my hands tightly together behind my back and waited to be dismissed. Instead, the General looked from the presentation to me and smiled. He said, "In all the years that we have done this exercise, no one has ever shared an approach like this, but it is valid, and probable. Nice job! You can have a seat." I smiled as if it were no big deal, replied, "Thank you, sir.", and took my seat with my heart threatening to jump out of my chest. My boss leaned back in his chair and whispered, "Wow! That was great! Not only was the information a new approach, but you delivered it like this was a fireside chat. Very enjoyable when we see so many of these." He gave me a huge smile, then turned back around to the next presenter.

Suffice it to say, that was definitely a good day! At the end of the military exercise, I was one of only two people to receive a reward from the General for my contribution.

Sadly, I did not learn my lesson until years later. I still tried to act like my male counterparts for years, intermittently having moments like this example on my journey to self-discovery. Carla Harris' pearl on authenticity helped to put things into perspective for me. Ultimately, the only way to leverage my strengths is to know who I am, how I prefer to approach things, and share my authentic self in my dealings. This approach is something I can sustain because it's me without pretense; me without embellishments; my unique self, warts, and all.

That's not easy for the 13 to 18-year-old group in many cases. Allyson V. captured this well by saying:

I think in middle school and high school the students who wanted to be leaders or involved in school activities were viewed as "not cool" and I think there is a lot of pressure to fit in at that age. There's a lot of herd mentality. For example, "I don't want to be different than my friends" or "my friends aren't doing that, so I am not going to do it".

It's difficult to be different when there is such a desire to fit in, to belong. However, the sooner you can accept and own who you are, the sooner you can feel comfortable in your own skin. The less stress and pressure you will feel to be something that you're not.

I like what Laurel T. shared that, "Extroverts may naturally be considered leaders more than Introverts simply because they are outgoing, and they speak up faster. But anyone can lead well." Whereas Darcy K. clarified that she "had the desire to lead when I was passionate about the subject. I led in the theater groups, and I led in English class. However, I did not lead in Science." This speaks to having a better understanding of self, and where you'll feel more confident when leading, basically what's important to you.

Also keep in mind that you may learn that you are not comfortable leading from the front. Leaders can serve from behind the scenes in many ways. You can be a top performer in a field, sport, or industry. Lisa C. offers her story:

I was spoiled, but I was also disciplined when I needed it. I had a happy go lucky childhood. Which is why I was always going with the flow, good or bad. My only goal was to party. It wasn't until I was just about out of high school when I started to wake up and realized, o lord, my mom doesn't have to do anything for me anymore if she chooses not to. So, although I had no clue as to what I wanted to do with my life, my mom said if I learned to type I could get a job anywhere. So, I learned to type. But one thing for sure is although I have some family members that are fantastic entrepreneurs I knew I was and wanted to be a worker bee. Everybody is not a chief, but the chief needs some Indians. As I progressed in my life I found that my calling was to be of service, which is why I am most comfortable in being a worker bee. And I am exceptionally good at my service.

So where can you start to better understand yourself? There is a myriad of self-assessment tools that are available to help gain a baseline understanding. I do warn against labeling a person based on the results of an assessment. That would mean that you can never change; that the person you are at 20 is the same at 40. Your preferences and communication styles may be, but continued education, exposure, and experiences help you to learn and adapt in different situations in a more sustainable way. Leveraging your strengths during the learning process is key.

I have experience with numerous assessments like Meyers Briggs, Keirsey Bates, DISC, etc. However, the one that I find most accessible, quick to complete, easy to understand, and consistently accurate is The Predictive Index. At my company, we have had an over 30 year relationship with PIMidlantic which trains our managers to understand the reports, and provides analytics to better understand the individuals we are hiring, and how they might fit into the dynamics of our teams and business culture. As anything, it is not 100% accurate, but offers an excellent gauge for initial insights.

Next you'll hear another perspective on this topic from Stephen Picarde. He is the Chief Executive Officer and Talent Optimization Specialist for PIMidlantic and is a leading authority on the Predictive Index (PI). Steve has been an important partner with my company in the use of the PI Assessment tool. The primary purpose initially was gaining insight for potential new hires. Today, Steve and his team have enhanced the online features to develop others, evaluate team dynamics, and more. Steve has forgotten more about PI than I have learned about it. Steve . . .

"Yesterday I was clever, so I wanted to change the world. Today I am wise, so I am changing myself." – Rumi

We are works in progress. Finding our way in the world, creating our place, learning what makes us unique, building the best version of us.

Self-awareness is a lifetime journey. Or it isn't Self-awareness is the ability to focus on yourself and how your actions, thoughts, or emotions do or don't align with your internal standards. If you're highly self-aware, you can objectively evaluate yourself, manage your emotions, align your behavior with your values, and understand correctly how others perceive you.

Dr. Tasha Eurich's, an organizational psychologist and sought-after keynote speaker, research suggests that 95% of people think they are self-aware, yet only 15% of people ARE self-aware. So, on any given day 80% of us are lying to ourselves about lying to ourselves.

Why try at all? People more self-aware are more fulfilled, have stronger relationships, perform better, and tend toward more job satisfaction.

The beginnings of self-awareness occur when we understand our natural preferences. What we prefer to do, NOT what we can do. We can do most of what we put our mind to, but that doesn't mean we're energized or motivated.

My own experience with self-awareness began when I was exploring careers and colleges. Like many, I had no firm idea of what area to pursue. I knew I tended to be good in sciences, so I thought I'd start there. Getting a course book from Northeastern University, I began thumbing through the majors.

Chemistry, interesting, but I need a master's degree. Biology, really enjoyable, but what do you do with it? Then I saw the next page, Pharmacy. I would get a job right out of college, be respected, and my mother would be happy that I'd have security. Thus, began a 5-year journey to a Pharmacy degree.

Indeed, once I graduated I had immediate job offers and moved to Maryland.

Starting the job was exciting, as there was a lot to learn. But quickly, I became dissatisfied, wondering where this would lead; it seemed repetitive and transactional. After a year I would stay up nights thinking is this what it will be like for the next 40 years? I would, at times, hate to see the sun come up.

I fortunately got into management, went to work for a consulting firm and started my own business 35 years ago. A much more fulfilling path.

Pharmacy is a great profession. One of the most trusted by consumers. Genuinely helps people. But it just wasn't for me.

So, I started doing what I should have done 8 years before, and reflected on what I enjoyed doing, what energized me, what environments were truly motivating. And conversely, what I didn't enjoy, what was an energy drain. I soon realized I had probably made a bad career choice, *for me*, and had a clearer vision of what I'd pursue in the future.

Some of this is self-selecting. Reserved, analytical, detail-oriented people may gravitate toward accounting, research, computer programming. Outgoing, freewheeling, independent people may gravitate towards sales or marketing.

The most important thing is You Be You. Understand what the best place for you is and don't try to be someone else's vision of you. Accept your likes and dislikes and grow from there.

While consulting, I was introduced to the Predictive Index. When I got the results I said, "This explains a lot." It was eye opening, and comforting. There was nothing wrong with me. I just wasn't going to enjoy the environment my prior job offered. I did it well, it just wasn't fulfilling. Understanding myself better, I pursued goals more in line with my strengths and went on to build the largest Predictive Index practice in the world.

You may benefit from creating an inventory list of your preferences. Then running it by people who know you for input.

Another way is to complete a behavioral assessment. There are many out there, for many different purposes. They will allow you to reflect on you.

I have used the Predictive Index for many years with businesses worldwide in the field of Talent Optimization, helping them maximize their most important asset.

At an extremely high level we measure people on a scale of 4 behavioral drives, we all have them, but to different extents. These are not the only four human behaviors, but simply ones that relate to business environments and personal relationships.

Below is a broad scale that you may see yourself and others in.

The Collaboration to Dominance Scale:

Dominance | Needs

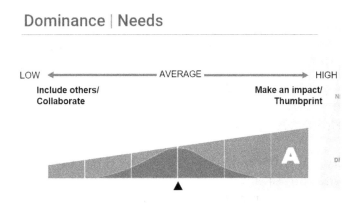

Those people more to the COLLABORATION side (left of scale) are the consummate team players, always doing things for others, very accommodating, seeking harmony in relationships, generally uncritical and easy going. They like sharing the risk with others. Collaborators may gravitate to roles where they help people, teachers, hospitality, customer service, professions

However, they typically don't like conflict and shy away from it. they often have a hard time saying no and take on more than they should. To avoid addressing issues directly they may do other people's jobs.

Those on the DOMINANCE side like to be in control of situations, they tend to be assertive, directive, and challenging, Winning is important, every contest, and every argument. Highly Dominant people are willing to step up and take charge when needed. They need lots of freedom and independence in their roles. They may gravitate toward leadership roles, entrepreneurial ventures, or where they can drive change.

However, when challenged they may attack. They believe they are right more often than not. They may judge people who are different harshly, and don't tend to get along with people who are similar for challenging them.

The Introversion to Extraversion Scale:

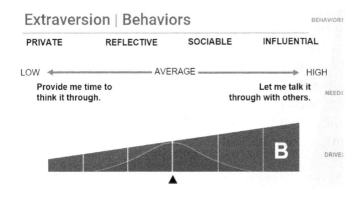

People to the left who are more INTROVERTED are often private and slow to open up. They are wary around new and unfamiliar people. Trust needs to be earned before they are comfortable. They anticipate problems and are very analytical. When they talk it's very businesslike and to the point. They enjoy their private time. Introverts often are attracted to fields where they work with things, accounting, computers, logistics, manufacturing

However, they may avoid or be less engaged in groups of unfamiliar people. They can be slow to open up and voice their opinions. Being analytical, they tend to point out what's wrong versus what's right. They may have fewer, but deeper, friendships. Introverts gravitate towards more "heads down jobs like Finance, Information Technology, data analysis, research, etc.

People to the EXTRAVERTED side walk into a room and fill it with charisma. They connect quickly with people and are generally optimistic. They excel at influencing people to their way of thinking. They may be spontaneous and at times have no filter when they speak. They want acceptance and for people to like them. Extraverts will gravitate towards Sales, client facing roles, public speaking etc.

However, in the extreme, their enthusiasm is best taken in small doses. They value being liked and may make promises they don't keep. They tend to want to be the center of attention and may be prone to exaggeration.

The Urgency to Patience Scale:

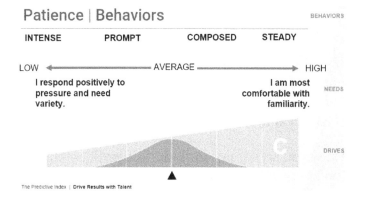

People toward the Urgency end of the scale have a lot of inner tension, and they want to release that tension in action. Do it now! They enjoy multitasking and want to see results from their efforts. Urgent people are self-starters and push themselves and others into action. They gravitate to roles where meeting deadlines and juggling tasks are rewarded.

However, Urgent people get bored by repetition, and in a process environment their mind wanders, and they may make simple mistakes. At times they are not the best listeners, try to finish the other people's sentences for them, and are prone to interrupting. They may gravitate towards roles like reporters, marketing, business development/sales, etc.

Individuals toward the Patient end of the scale pride themselves on being relaxed and calm in any situation. They are consistent and content with who they are. Patient people possess the ability to focus. They can concentrate for long periods of time. They generally possess a diplomatic nature and rarely make waves. They are drawn to roles such as accountants, surgeons, teachers, pharmacists, and diplomats.

However, someone who is very content defaults to the status quo. They don't tend to like change. At times they need to be pushed into action. Because of their ability to focus, they often miss deadlines when handling multiple priorities.

The Informal to Formal Scale:

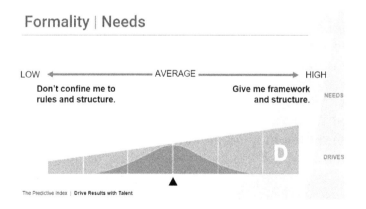

Formality | Needs

LOW ← AVERAGE → HIGH

Don't confine me to rules and structure.

Give me framework and structure.

NEEDS

D

DRIVES

The Predictive Index | Drive Results with Talent

People toward the informal scale tend to be very freewheeling and fearless. They view risk as opportunity and are challenged by it. They think in the big picture, possibilities, often neglecting to consider the details. Their mind seeks to change or improve situations rarely maintain them. They often act very spontaneously with little need for facts and information. They are found in sales, marketing, creative roles, and as entrepreneurs.

However, because they think in the big picture, details may fall through the cracks and are considered unimportant. At times, they speak with no filter, what comes in their head, comes out their mouth. Change is exciting and they may gravitate to change for the sake of change.

Highly Formal people are driven to conform to the established policies. They do it 'right'. They worry. They want and need all the information. Knowledge is power to the high Formal person. Worried about mistakes, they take great pains to mitigate risk. If you want it done right, give it to a formal person. They are experts, professionals, many times in narrowly focused specialties.

However, because they worry about doing it right, Highly Formal people tend not to delegate to others and do it all themselves. They tend to be perfectionists where good is never good enough and they spend an inordinate time on the last 10%.

Perhaps when you read these you related some traits to yourself and your friends and family. You may have these *preferences*. You can do whatever you want, but these areas seem to engage you more than the others

Many people spend much of their time trying to put in what they feel God left out. It's a better strategy to hone your strengths. However, push yourself out of your comfort zone now and then. This is how we grow.

If you're Introverted, you may be uncomfortable going to social events alone and meeting new people. You're not defective, this is how you were built. So put a date on the calendar and give an event a try. You may find it isn't so bad, or it may reinforce it's not what you want to do. The important thing is that because others may like it doesn't mean it's right for you.

Understanding yourself builds a level of comfort. You don't have to be like others. You have skills that they don't. Be the best YOU that you can be. This is how you can find your passion, where you can add value, how you can be useful in your own way.

When I was first introduced to the Predictive Index, I realized how helpful a tool it could be to young adults. While learning to be a practitioner of its use, I was encouraged to use it as much as possible. So, I ran mini workshops with young women to not only practice but test my theory that understanding oneself earlier from a positive perspective can drive them to create a plan for themselves that presents opportunity for positive outcomes. It was a resounding success! The participants expressed feeling more in control of choosing the direction of their future plans, and the leaders of these young women's programs have frequently asked for me to return to work with the next groups. Although this is not the only tool available and by no means a "silver bullet", anything that encourages confidence in a young woman at a time in their lives when they tend to struggle with it, helps.

#JUSTBEME

ACTIVITY PAGE

Change your mindset. Instead of asking WHY (why did this happen to me? Why doesn't she like me?) ask WHAT. What can I do so this doesn't happen next time? What do I need to do to make the team? Pick a recent issue that you experienced and apply this approach. Write the new WHAT question. (This step will apply to the next question to practice the new approach.)

_____

_____

_____

_____

_____

What results do you expect to see with this new approach to changing your mindset?

_____

_____

_____

_____

_____

_____

_____

_____

APPLICATION

Reflect on yourself. What makes you happiest? What do you gravitate toward? What sucks your energy? Keep an inventory, pursue what makes you a better you.

_____

_____

_____

_____

_____

_____

_____

_____

_____

_____

_____

_____

_____

_____

_____

_____

_____

_____

_____

_____

CHAPTER 4

Needs & Wants (Priorities/ Time Management)

pri·or·i·ties
/prīˈôrədēz/

the areas of our lives that are meaningful and important to us.

If you're not clear on your **priorities**, you'll have trouble managing your time and making progress on your goals. This means **knowing the difference between needs and wants**. Needs are things that you want, but also must have to survive, such as food, water, shelter from the elements, etc. Wants are nice to have but aren't necessary. For instance, I NEED shoes to protect my feet, but I may WANT a particular name brand shoe. When you recognize the difference, it's easier to prioritize. It doesn't mean you can't include wants on occasion, but when you understand what is more important in the scheme of things, delayed gratification becomes easier because the ultimate goal you are trying to accomplish rises to the number one priority position. I call this your "super why". I created this term to capture the utmost important reason to help motivate you to maintain your priorities and stay on track when distractions and disruptions block your progress. Therefore, time management is so critical to your success. Without it, it would be difficult to fit all that is required in the day for the average high school student. Distractions will only make it worse. Let's take a closer look at this.

I thought my days were busy in the early 80's. I got up at 5:30 am to walk our dog, Misty. Then I packed me and my siblings lunches for school, caught the bus, attended class all day, most of which were advanced (which was not the norm for most students at that time), participated in a gifted program, reported to Track & Field practice or competitions after school (not to mention the often weekend competitions), got a ride home or to my job (As soon as I could, I always seemed to have a job. I was a newspaper delivery girl and baby sitter at first, then I became a telemarketer selling Olan Mills portrait packages at 16, then later was a Retail Sales Associate and Stock Clerk for Show Off, a discount retail clothing store when I was 17 - 18), completed my homework, went to bed, and started over the next weekday. Sounds pretty busy, right?

Then I watched my daughters attend high school from 2007 – 2013. I honestly don't know how they did it except pure ingenuity. My oldest daughter had my schedule, but also added high school Lacrosse Goalie, Forensics/Debate, Mock Government competitions, and worked at a local bookstore. She also joined Toastmasters with my husband at the local library. Add to this, she has always had an entrepreneurial spirit and started a few online businesses pertaining to sale and resale of items on the internet. The middle child, chose not to work other than a little babysitting on occasion, but took more AP classes than I would expect anyone to do on purpose while she trained year-round to become a top state high school athlete in long distance, spent her summers studying Calculus or traveling abroad, or attending summer programs on how to be a Global Citizen, or going to The Governor's School, and, and,

and . . . I'm not certain that I would have been as successful as them in this generation when everyone is so academically competitive while many students were making choices to strengthen their resumes to go to their colleges of choice.

This isn't meant to be a story about my family and how busy we are. It's meant to let you know that you are not alone with life's hectic ways and how overwhelming it can get. Sometimes it can feel that way, but remember **you are not alone**. What follows are some examples on how to manage your priorities and time more effectively but connecting with other like-minded students can also help.

Ultimately, what my daughters, and many of their friends, chose to do was to focus on the things that were the **most important to their personal goals**. It let them allocate the time accordingly.

As I observed their approach to managing their priorities and time, I had a flash-back. My biggest concern about their schedules was maintaining **balance**. Personally, as a high school student, I tended to not find the time to associate with others on a social level. It wasn't that I didn't want to, but I frequently put the functional before the fun, and would often run out of time before the fun would occur. So, I tried to make certain that my girls made time for things that they felt were just for fun because I didn't want them to make the same mistake that I did. Although I was well-rounded when it came to academics, athletics, leadership of different organizations, and enjoyed fun and support from my family, I didn't have many close friends in high school. To be honest, I only had one, Cathy C., in a school with over 2,000 students I knew other students through sports and clubs, but we didn't have a close bond, and I find that sad. I didn't have a birthday party with friends until I was 32 (Thanks, Tyno!). I didn't have a sleep-over with a friend until I was in my 40's (Thanks, Trudy!). I didn't really learn to socialize and read people and social cues effectively until I was in college for a couple of years. College gave me multiple "besties" (Melody, Kim, Trudy, Jane, Jayne, Tamara, to name a few), but I often wonder if I missed out on key high school experiences by not getting closer to my classmates sooner.

Don't get me wrong! I don't regret my choices. These were choices I made because I was determined to achieve my goals, and they shaped who I am today, and I like who I've become, but I didn't often take the time to enjoy just being a kid. I wanted a more balanced path for my daughters, so I tried to make sure to include social opportunities for them along with the more functional areas.

Balance is important. It doesn't have to be all or nothing, but it is important to keep in mind **what's most important to you**. If you want a successful future, delayed gratification may be something you'll need to practice on occasion. It means choosing to complete assignments before going to hang out with your friends. It means that time with your boyfriend may have to be scheduled. It also means not getting too serious about a boyfriend until you've accomplished some of your most important goals. You just need to determine your "super why". It's that ultimate reason that drives you to achieve something. For me, it was getting into the college of my choice with a scholarship so that my parents wouldn't need to help me pay for it, and I wouldn't have a huge debt as I started my first career. But yours could be anything. Prioritize and focus, and that dream can be yours when you keep your "super why" in front of you. It will help choose the needs over the wants to stay on track.

To exemplify this, here is a shared perspective on the importance of setting priorities and time management, as well as some examples of how this person does it. I have invested in and watched this young lady successfully implement them in school, career, and life.

When Nicole C. graduated from high school, she chose to attend a military academy for college. Her interest in foreign cultures motivated her to study French and Arabic and introduced her to a love for travelling abroad. As an avid runner, she also made time to prepare to run competitively in several half marathons, and both the New York and Boston marathons.

From this short bio alone, you can see that she was able to maintain a balance of the things that she felt were meaningful to her academic and personal life. Here's her perspective on how she did it.

Balance. There is no singular definition of it. Achieving balance is truly dependent upon one's priorities.

To start maintaining a more balanced life, I recommend sitting down and making a list of short-term and long-term goals. These can be spiritual, financial, social, fitness, etc. Once you have your goals, you know your priorities! You would not make goals for things you don't care about. However, you may want to rank them as an additional step.

Next step: examine your schedule. Where do you put most of your time and energy? Maybe you are being inefficient by giving your time to people that do not support your goals. Or maybe you spend a little too much time watching television, listening to just one more true crime podcast, or scrolling through social media. Either way, there are distractions in your life that will cause you to be less fervent in achieving your goals. Write down a list of these distractions so you are cognizant of them.

The final step is to make a plan. Make sure your plan is time-based and as detailed as possible!

For example, let's say you want to read more. "Reading more" is different for everyone, so let's say for you it's reading two books each month. The first step you can take is creating a reading list, so you have books at the ready to indulge in this task. Another step you can take is planning how many pages you will read each day, so you stay on track in completing your goal. But it's all up to you. Your goals, priorities, and balance are yours for the choosing.

This is only one way to approach prioritizing and managing your time. Maybe you're not a planner, and spontaneity is your preference. Choosing a more creative way to focus on the things that are the most meaningful to you will also work. It's up to you HOW you do it, but you will need to identify what you need and/or want and recognize when distractions are keeping you from achieving them. If you keep your "super why" in mind, it will often keep or help you get back on track.

So, what is a "super why"? It's your ultimate goal. It drives your key decisions. It gives you a singular focus when it's that important to you and your plans. For me, in my teens, it was about going to college. I'd be the first woman in the family to graduate from a 4-year college. However, I didn't want just any college. I wanted to go to a highly accredited college on a scholarship so that my parents wouldn't need to take on any debt for me to get a quality education. For me, it wasn't a matter of if, but when and how I'd accomplish this. That singular focus served me well.

But it's not just about your own needs and wants. One survey taker offered this poignant message:

I always wanted to be "in charge". I was the captain for my majorette team, president of my sorority, but I didn't understand what leadership meant. At that age I thought leadership was about making all the decisions, so that was appealing. By the time I was a teen I was tired of NOT being able to make my own decisions. I had not encountered leadership or mentors that did collaboration involving my wants in the final decision. So as a leader, I don't think I excelled. It wasn't until later in life when I had learned that leadership isn't about making all the decisions, it is more about the needs and wants of those who you lead."

It's important for us to remember that we are leading others so it's not about me, myself, and I. What you decide and do impacts them, so it may be beneficial to include them in the decision-making process when and where it makes sense.

Now let's look at how you can practice prioritizing and managing your time as a leader with the following activities.

#WIN

ACTIVITY PAGE

What is your "super why"? Dig deep to avoid being superficial.

_____

_____

_____

_____

_____

_____

_____

_____

_____

List your needs and wants, then prioritize them.

_____

_____

_____

_____

_____

_____

_____

_____

_____

_____

_____

APPLICATION

What are some strategies that you plan to use to remind yourself of your "super why" when you should choose delayed gratification, needs over wants, or the functional before the fun? This exercise is best conducted with the guidance of a mentor to advise on different strategies (e.g. Guidance Counselor).

_____

_____

_____

_____

_____

_____

_____

_____

_____

_____

_____

_____

_____

_____

_____

_____

_____

_____

CHAPTER 5

Know Stuff

con·tin·u·ous learn·ing
/kənˈtinyo͞oəs/ /ˈlərniNG/

the ongoing gaining of knowledge or skills through
experience, study, by being modeled or mentored

There is always more that you can learn, even when you are considered an expert in your field. I've been able to be a credible resource of information as a Human Resources professional for numerous years, but I consistently recognize that there is still so much that I can learn to hone my skills to help others. So much so, that I have decided to return to school to continue my education. However, if you'd asked me if I had wanted an advanced degree when I had completed my BS in General Engineering, I would have told you that you were crazy. I honestly felt that an undergraduate degree was more than enough to compete for future roles or give me a baseline of knowledge as a springboard without the need for additional education. Then I discovered a career passion that made me want to know more. Made me want to be better. Made me want to invest in others to achieve their potential. Experience, education, reading, and role models continue to play a huge part in my continuous learning journey to achieve that elusive "I have arrived" moment. I think if I do have that moment, it may be time to move onto something else.

Not everyone wants to follow this type of path. Some aren't interested in a continued formal education. Since that is the case, and many have become successful without a degree, how did they do it? Add to that, why did they do it the way that they did? What inspired them to choose the paths that they chose?

When my husband and I had children, we viewed a quality education as a must to ensure that they were not disadvantaged from meeting their long-term career goals (or the ones we pictured for them). This was, of course, before we learned who our children were as people with desires, goals, and aspirations of their own, along with an independent view of how best to get there. But that's the thing, isn't it? There is no one way to learn how to get where you want to go. That's the million-dollar question. Which path is best for me? Hopefully, this chapter will offer some insights that match best to your approach to learning, and that you choose never to stop investing in yourself in all the ways that you like to learn.

To start a continuous learning journey, it's helpful to understand your preferred learning style. Although your preference may not fit neatly into one of these categories, most fall into one of the following four styles:

- Visual
- Auditory
- Kinesthetic
- Reading/Writing

Techworld Language Solutions at techworldinc. com provides a high-level understanding of the preferences for each. Keep in mind that the most effective learning will consist of a combination of learning styles as it will encourage improved retention of the information that is shared.

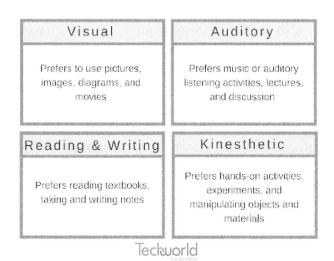

Visual	Auditory
Prefers to use pictures, images, diagrams, and movies	Prefers music or auditory listening activities, lectures, and discussion
Reading & Writing	Kinesthetic
Prefers reading textbooks, taking and writing notes	Prefers hands-on activities, experiments, and manipulating objects and materials

Teckworld

Once you have a better understanding of your learning style, you can search for programs, courses, workshops, certifications, etc. that offer course materials and a format that includes methods that speak to your preferred learning style.

You can also learn by teaching others. With this approach, you can gain additional and more detailed knowledge on a topic as you prepare to answer the variety of questions of participants. The different perspectives help to increase your understanding of that specific topic. When you can clearly communicate knowledge about a subject, and consistently reach each learner at his/her level, you will be a credible resource of information.

In addition to my perspective, I wanted Dr. Victoria Jones to share her insights on the importance and impact of continuous learning. Dr. Jones was the Director of Learning & Development at General Motors University (GMU) when I worked there. I have admired her accomplishments to include her return to school to get her Ph.D. Over the years, she, along with Nancy, became my friend as well as mentor. Her perspective here offers understanding of the impactful learning can be.

It was a fall afternoon and an invitation had been extended to do a workshop regarding the importance of teamwork. This was an outreach project to make a difference in a local community. The audience was a group of high schoolers enrolled in Thurston High School located in Redford, Michigan. Participants were eager to learn about teamwork and how it might make a difference and have impact.

The workshop centered on a group exercise titled the Marshmallow Challenge.

The purpose of the Marshmallow Challenge was to build knowledge related to the importance of teamwork in building collaborative relationships. As these students were thinking about college upon completing high school, knowing about teamwork dynamics would become critically important. The Marshmallow Challenge is a kinesthetic exercise providing hands on experimentation through group engagement.

For example, group projects serve as an essential method of learning in a college setting. Knowing how to optimize the relationship building process sets the stage for authentic teamwork. Knowing that collaboration is a method to move from a good project or outcome to a great one.

Students were divided into teams of 5 and there were five teams for a total of 25 participants. Each team collected a building kit comprised of 20 sticks of spaghetti, one yard of tape, one yard of string, and one marshmallow.

The following directions were provided to the teams as the challenge:

1. Build the tallest free-standing structure in 18 minutes or less, using materials found in the building kit. Additional materials could not be added.

2. The marshmallow must be on top of the structure

3. The expectation was for all members of the team to contribute to the building process

4. The structure must stand without collapsing at the end of the exercise

5. The winner of the Marshmallow Challenge would be the team with the tallest free-standing structure

Students had fun with the Marshmallow Challenge and a winner emerged. Engagement was high among most students; however, some choose to watch rather than participate. Students shared important lessons learned and new knowledge from the Challenge:

1. An enhanced appreciation for listening to the ideas of others

2. Clear communication is vital in development understanding

3. Collaboration is essential in working with others

4. Assumptions can get in the way of success

5. Work to create an inclusive environment is important—all voices should be heard

6. It is acceptable to have trial and error along the way rather than testing near the end of time parameters

In closing, the debrief from the experiment at Thurston High School represents essentials of knowing the importance of teamwork:

Clearly, learning about the importance of teamwork is only one example, but it is one that can help navigate any group efforts. The reason this lesson

learned is so impactful is because it's important to remember that you are not alone, and that collaboration can make for better outcomes.

As you gain more knowledge and experience, you will more than likely gain more responsibility. However, keep in mind that "to whom much is given, much will be expected". But don't worry. You've got this!

Also keep in mind that all learning is good learning. In addition to learning how to correctly do things, you may discover what to avoid in the future, or whose leadership style you don't want to model. It all can contribute to your betterment. So, take the good with the not so good learning moments and apply them too.

Having said that, let's take a closer look at how you learn and what you'd like to learn more about in the following activities.

#LIFELONGLEARNING

ACTIVITY PAGE

What is your preferred learning style? Why do you believe that? Make sure to tie it back to the definition of the learning style.

_____
_____
_____
_____
_____
_____
_____
_____

What are you most interested in? What could you learn more about to improve in this area of interest? Where or from whom can you gain access to this information to learn more?

_____
_____
_____
_____
_____
_____
_____
_____

APPLICATION

Based on the area of interest in the previous activity, seek this new knowledge and apply it. Upon completion, note how the gaining of new knowledge impacted how you later viewed the area of interest.

_____

_____

_____

_____

_____

_____

_____

_____

_____

_____

_____

_____

_____

_____

_____

_____

_____

_____

_____

_____

CHAPTER 6

Stronger than you Think (Strength, Determination, & Perseverance)

strength
/streNG(k)TH/

is a person's capacity to withstand pressure

de·ter·mi·na·tion
/dəˌtərməˈnāSH(ə)n/

is a firmness of purpose, or resolve;
resoluteness

per·se·ver·ance
/pərsəˈvirəns/

is the continued effort to do or achieve something
despite difficulties, failure, or opposition.

Have you ever doubted your ability to do something difficult? Before trying something new or different, you talked yourself out of it. Self-doubt is something that we all experience at some point in time, especially when the task at hand is daunting, or the first time you've been exposed to a situation. However, when you stop to think what can be gained by accomplishing it, if the perceived outcome outweighs the expected effort, some will take that leap of faith. For each person who does, strength, determination, and perseverance will be exhibited. Each situation may require more or less of each characteristic, but will access them, nonetheless.

I have found that understanding others' experiences and trials have been extremely helpful when determining what approach that I take; multiple experiences offer multiple options to consider. Comparing and contrasting, or just seeking inspiration tends to solidify in my mind what will work for me. The next stories are an example of what I'm speaking of.

Udon C. is the Sprint Coach at East Carolina University (ECU). The road to this role was a winding one full of detours and roadblocks, but he made it, and his future is bright. His story below in his own words occurred at the start of his journey on that road to being a sought-after Track & Field Coach.

When I was a freshman in college, I got up nearly every weekday morning to go on a long run before I showered and went to class. I'd go out for 16 minutes, and wherever I was at that point, I would turn around and try to come back in 14 minutes. My coach didn't tell me to do it. My lack of a scholarship told me to do it. I was a walk-on at East Carolina University.

I also did at least 500 extra abs exercises a day in addition to what we were already doing in the weight room. I studied on the floor and stretched while I read my textbooks. I stayed after practice and did drills. Again, no one told me to do it. My lack of a scholarship told me to do it. I was obsessed.

My father had told me if I didn't get a scholarship after my first year that I'd have to come home. After the first year, despite all the hard work, I didn't get a scholarship, so my father stayed true to his word. I had to come home. It was heartbreaking.

During that time, I probably worked out harder than I've ever worked in my life. I had a job and I did two-a-days. I can't begin to tell you how many abs I did because I'd do abs or push-ups through every commercial break when I watched television in the evening. My friend, Todd R., gave me a training regimen to follow, and I followed it to the letter. I wanted to be ready when I had saved enough money to go back to ECU.

Well, it wasn't looking like I was going to make it financially to return to college, so Todd convinced me to ask his coach, John Cook (Head Coach of George Mason), to transfer there. Coach Cook called my coach (Bill Carson of ECU), and when Coach Carson found out that Coach Cook wanted me, he asked me if I'd come back for a 50% scholarship. I had saved up a little over 50% on my own, so I accepted, and the rest is history.

I came back and went from being a walk-on with a time of 50 seconds in the open 400m to a time of 46-high, a drop of over 3 seconds for this short distance. This effort also improved my 400m hurdle time to 51-high. I even earned a little more (scholarship-wise) before I finished.

I say all this to say that if you want something bad enough, you can get it. You just have to pin your ears back and put the work in.

Another example of determination and perseverance is from Jasmyn M. When looking through the comments shared in the survey, I was intrigued by her responses to a couple of the questions pertaining to never giving up, and no being temporary although she still struggles with it. So, I reached out to interview her further. Here's her story:

When growing up, I never realized that my family was poor. I was actually pretty spoiled. My mother would put a spin on things in such a way that I thought leaving the oven door open after meals to heat the house, or using candles for lighting were not only normal, but fun.

I remember asking my mother for something this one time when I usually got my way, and I took it pretty hard. But then she said, "Jasmyn, the word 'no' is only temporary. When one door closes, another opens." I adopted this philosophy. Things come in God's timing. Sometimes the answer is just 'not right now. When the current answer is 'no', it's important to include an explanation. That seems so final. However, if the reason is understood, this now becomes an option.

I'll admit that I still struggle with it. We are human, so hearing 'no' still hurts. It can feel deflating and isn't easy to hear. It makes you want to try to fix it quickly to get back to 'yes'. But I quickly get back to that philosophy that "No is only temporary".

I expect that you can relate and add your story for facing a difficult situation and pushing through. I know that this philosophy has worked for me. I don't tend to immediately reply with no when asked for help. It's important to consider all options. However, if you end up saying no, all involved understand that we've explored all the options and ended up with the best solution for now.

When you apply this mindset and a more mindful approach to each difficult situation, the outcome will tend to be more positive. Here's another example of how Angela S. was able to remain determined and to persevere despite others not believing in her:

I remember sitting in the auditorium at the end of my Freshman year of high school and watching Michelle R. get the Best Female Athlete of the Year. I said out loud, with no reservations, I would get The Best Female Athlete of the Year as a graduating senior. I was sitting with the track team, and they all started laughing, because I hadn't run well all season. So, all that summer I ran every day, improving on my speed and endurance. I did hundreds of sit-ups a day, several times a day. I came back to school in fantastic shape and decided to run cross country. My very first race, I won! As I became a better athlete, I also became a more disciplined student. I worked hard in and out of the classroom, and it paid off over the last three years of my high school career. I let the laughter of the track team fuel my desire to be the best that I could be. I felt no pressure from anyone but me to always do my absolute best, and if I failed, it would be another challenge to rise to the occasion on another day. I learned to listen to myself, and every time I wanted to stop, I would ask, "I thought you wanted to be the best?" I would tell myself that someone somewhere was working as hard or harder than me to win. The questions I asked myself allowed me to persevere. I utilized the same perseverance and discipline to start businesses, purchase properties, and become dedicated to mentoring other young women. I let those young women know that life will happen, disappointments will come, there will be failures, but if you don't give up, there will be successes. Set your goals high and work at achieving them, PERIOD. Hard work allowed me to have a choice of where I went to college; my athleticism and academics gave me the privilege of choice. I believed that all things were possible through Christ who strengthened me. I did the work, and I continue to do the work. From humble beginnings in track and field to Female Athlete of The Year 1985, I'm still pursuing and persevering regardless of circumstances.

Note that Angela claimed the results 3 years prior to the results coming to fruition. This was her "super why" (covered in Chapter 5), and she continued her efforts to achieve her goal with determination and perseverance despite others not believing that she could do it.

I'd like to end this chapter with an inspirational story about a young lady who has challenges that she has worked hard to overcome. Most weren't even aware that she struggled with anything serious. The first that any of us discovered how trying her journey has been was when she spoke at church prior to her graduation. You see, the

Youth Pastor invites a deserving senior to speak before the congregation about something inspiring. The student is a mystery guest. Often the parents and family are surprised when they discover who the speaker is. Here is most of her speech as the surprise guest, titled 'Be Fearless':

The reason why the title is called fearless is because fearless means to be not afraid of taking chances, it also means to be strong and not afraid of anything. Fearless is such a powerful word because it shows how strong and mighty God is. Also, it shows how You can do anything if you put your mind to it!

It doesn't matter if you're different. I doesn't matter if you look or sound different. That's who you are. You were born that way. That's what God created you to be and you can't be scared of yourself. Yes, you can get scared about little things but, the one thing you can't get scared of is yourself. It's ok be yourself because it's you

To be honest, we all have things that we are all afraid off such as snakes or bugs. A lot of us have something that we're afraid of but you can't be afraid of things that stand in your way. We all must stand up and be a strong as children of God, and push through the giant walls that block our paths.

I only have one point in this sermon it's a quote from Denzel Washington's graduation speech and it says, "Put God first."

If you guys didn't know, I was born with learning disabilities called auditory processing disorder and ADHD without the hyperactivity. Throughout the years in school, I had problems with my reading, writing comprehension, and Math reasoning. My teacher noticed that I couldn't comprehend everything with the other kids in class. Eventually I was given all types of testing. The Principal at the time refused to hold me back a grade. I went through test after test after test.

One of the reasons why I have a learning disability was that I was born prematurely, weighing only 3lbs and 7 ounces. Now as a graduating senior, I understand how to handle my disability with discipline. My disorder brought me where I am today. There were days that I thought I was never gonna make it. Now I'm graduating and I remember to put God first in every situation that I go through. Putting God first will help you go through anything that your stressing over. It can be in school, on your job or in family situations. Just put God first.

To all the young people that are still in school, remember, we are not perfect! I was born with a disorder and a learning disability, and I'm not perfect. We all go through things and some people want to be perfect so that they can tear you down because they think you they're 'all that'. Remember to don't be like those people and don't try to impress people to get what you want. Just be yourself and stay positive to protect your dreams!

Don't let fear stop you doing the things you love. Just be happy with your life, enjoy the life God gave you. Also, thank God for your life, for your parents, for your siblings, for the house you live in, food on the table, clothes, shoes. Not many have what we have today. Because you only get one chance and one opportunity to live your life! So, use it because, I believe that you all can!
    Thank you

I certainly didn't realize that Faith had so many hurdles. I often saw her sing solos, participate in drama events, and become the youth President despite being painfully shy. I personally thought that overcoming this alone was a fete. Then to find out that she successfully and privately fought through these additional struggles . . . . Call me impressed! I shed a tear or two that day. Not only for her, but other young women who struggle to make their mark, but don't choose a fearless approach, or have a family as supportive as Faith's, or a Principal who didn't give up, believing that she belonged in the grade that she was in. We don't live our lives alone, so there is no need to struggle alone.

After the next exercise, the following chapter will speak to this. In the meantime, let's practice what you've learned in this chapter.

#STRONGER

<u>ACTIVITY PAGE</u>

What is your biggest challenge or difficult goal to reach that you wish to attain?

_____

_____

_____

_____

_____

_____

_____

_____

What are the perceived roadblocks to conquering the challenge of accomplishing this goal successfully?

_____

_____

_____

_____

_____

_____

_____

_____

_____

_____

APPLICATION

For every roadblock that you've listed above, brainstorm ways to break the barriers.

_____

_____

_____

_____

_____

_____

_____

_____

_____

_____

_____

_____

_____

_____

_____

_____

_____

_____

_____

_____

_____

CHAPTER 7

You're Not Alone (Coach, Mentor, & Support)

coach
/kōCH/

men·tor
/menˌtər/

*(My definitions of a good coach and mentor
are noted at the beginning of the chapter.)*

What's the difference between a Coach and a Mentor? I'd say one is more for day to day guidance, and the other has a long-term focus/impact. Let's first define each to understand why they are different.

Coach - A good coach focuses on identifying goals, prioritizing them, and choosing the right path to achieve them. In doing so, coaches help you become more accountable, goal-driven, and competitive.

Mentor - A good mentor is experienced and provides support to protégés about their overall growth and interpersonal skill development. Specifically, a mentor helps protégés explore options, set development goals, develop new contacts and networks, and identify resources needed for their growth. In this way, a mentor serves as a trusted advisor and role model for protégés.

Coaching tends to offer day-to-day suggestions for the protégé to stay on track to meet long-term goals, whereas mentoring provides support that is directionally correct toward an overall vision. Sometimes the protégé can't quite articulate a vision. In this case, engaging with a mentor (or mentors) can help a protégé better define his or her own vision through interaction with a role model.

Remember the story in the previous chapter on how Udon C. showed strength, determination, and perseverance to accomplish a goal. What I didn't share previously is that he had a supportive friend who filed the role of coach and made a significant impact on achieving his goal of returning to ECU. Here is the rest of the story:

I owe a major debt to Todd R. for sticking by my side and sticking up for me. If it hadn't been for the elite training program he gave me over that period of time I don't know if my archaic plan would've worked. I was just going on long runs and smashing hills. But one thing is for sure. I wanted it, I went after it and I got it.

How bad do you want it? Do you have someone to count on to help you get it? You might want to find that someone. We weren't meant to do life alone. Thanks Todd. I couldn't have done it without you.

It was Todd's immediate guidance, or coaching, that put him on the right path to accomplishing his goal.

I'll never forget one of the coaching moments that I received from my first Director, Mary T., when working for GMU. We had a quarterly check-in scheduled. Mary started with the positive things that I had been doing, then mentioned a few areas for improvement that she thought would help me be more successful. The one item that stood out to me most was about an email I had sent to a customer. Mary noted that I had jumped right into the message without a greeting. I had been so focused on what I needed to do, that I didn't take the time to connect with the person on the other end of the message. She also suggested that I should use "I" statements for accountability, and "we" statements to share successful accomplishments. I've never forgotten that coaching moment, and every time I write an email, I re-read it and modify it to reflect what I learned. I still sometimes forget the greeting during the initial draft because my nature is to be focused on the mission at hand, but re-reading allows me to fix it before I send it out. I also re-read to make sure to share successes with my team because I recognize that I can't go it alone. More synergy and dynamic results come from multiple perspectives, and I enjoy giving kudos where they are deserved. The appreciation of the team tends to result in their not hesitating to contribute further in the future.

I have had multiple coaches and mentors throughout my youth and adult life. Some have supported me in both capacities. One such person was Mary's replacement, Nancy Bennett. She continued to invest in my operational growth as my Manager and coach at GMU and prepared me for a new and broader role within HR. However, we continued to stay connected after I moved on, and even after she left the company. To this day, I still reach out to her as a mentor because I value her opinion as a trusted advisor. So much so, that I've asked her to offer her voice as another perspective on this topic.

Nancy is not only my Mentor, but also my friend since we've known each other for about 15 years. She credits her success in life to the people who coached and mentored her during her childhood and early career beginning with her Japanese mother, who taught her at an early age. This set the stage for her desire to learn, grow, and succeed Professionally.

Nancy's perspective on coaching and mentoring has been impacted by her personal experiences being coached and mentored by others, and as a result, impacted me. In her words…

The people who coached and mentored me as a young woman had no special training or titles; they were simply good teachers who cared about their students and wanted us to succeed. I was fortunate enough to be one of the young people they took an interest in: Mrs. Dent, my first grade teacher, who finally gave in to my daily pestering for homework, and assigned me more challenging work to do after school, igniting my lifelong love for learning; Mr. Smith, our school's basketball coach, who taught me that the best things in life are worth working hard for, to learn from my mistakes, and not to give up when things get tough, and Mr. Pugh, my high school English teacher and our school's cross country coach, who inspired me with his optimism and resilience after a cycling accident left him paralyzed, who taught me about facing life's obstacles with grace and courage and that it is crucial to make each moment count as we never know what tomorrow may bring. Each of those special teachers shared something unique that changed my life, and as a girl from a low income, working class home with parents (dad, mom, and stepmom) who had not graduated from high school, they inspired me to reach for the stars and pursue my dreams.

There are potential coaches and mentors all around you. Some will seek you out; some you will find. Some will be easy to identify because of their title, like your softball coach, while others may happen because of a hobby, activity, the neighborhood you live in, or the community center where you volunteer or hang out.

What can you expect from a coach or mentor? That will depend on what you need. A coach is typically someone from whom you will receive advice on how to improve your performance on a specific task or in a particular area such as sharpening your tennis backhand or strengthening your writing or presentation skills. It's usually short-term (e.g. for the sports season). A coach will identify and help you build upon your strengths and improve upon weaknesses related to what you're seeking to get better at, will focus you on a specific goal or challenge, and will help you achieve it. Research shows that for young people who are at risk for falling off track, mentoring has these benefits (vs. their peers): 55% less likely to miss a day of school, 55% more likely to be in college, 46% less likely to start using drugs, and 81% more likely to participate in sports or school extracurriculars (*Mentoring,* Mentor.org).

A mentor relationship tends to be longer (weeks, months, or even years) and their purpose is to guide and support you in your personal or career development. A mentor will be a source of wisdom and experience as you prepare for college, figure out what field you want to study, or deal with personal challenges such as academic problems, bullying, or peer conflicts. A mentor often begins by helping you learn about yourself, what makes you unique and special, and what you are most passionate about. They may ask what things you've done or tried that excited or bored you, what things/school subjects are easy or hard for you, and what do you want to learn more about or never study again? They may suggest you take an assessment like the Myers-Briggs Type Indicator (MBTI) or Tom Rath's StrengthsFinder 2.0. The findings from those instruments, and your conversations with your mentor, can help you build your personal brand and articulate a clear vision for your life by identifying what you enjoy most, what frustrates you, and what types of jobs or professions would be most rewarding for you. Mentors can help you develop people skills by advising you on how to effectively handle and resolve conflicts with parents, other adults, and peers; resist "negative talk" and promote team spirit or positive personal relationships; or figure out how to get things done, beyond the organization chart, at the company where you have a part-time or summer job. They will ask you questions, challenge your thinking, listen to you, and push you out of your comfort zone when that will help you grow or learn. A mentor may also recommend you seek coaching or advice from others who are experts in areas they are not, such as a math tutor or a counselor for depression. Even if you pursue help from someone else on a specific matter, your mentor often remains accessible to you as your guide and supporter.

My advice is to be bold and ask for help, direction, and advice when you need it. And, be patient. Some people will connect with you while others will not. Don't be discouraged if a person you have approached seems not to have the type of help you're seeking or the time to spend with you. Learn what you can and move on. Take advantage of teachers when you need coaching on a specific academic subject – some may even be available to tutor you; approach your sports coach for advice about how to improve your athletic performance; and seek out adults around you who have experience in a field you're interested in like medicine, social media, law, social activism, fashion, or journalism. You may be surprised how willing adults are to share their experience with you. Be open to the possibilities as you never know what will bear fruit in the future. Think about Steve Jobs, the co-founder of Apple Computer. When he was a young man, he audited a college course on Calligraphy, not because he especially wanted to learn this ancient writing art, but he thought it sounded interesting. Later, he was inspired by what he'd learned in that calligraphy course to invent the creative fonts used on his Apple computers. Great ideas can come from the most unexpected places (and people).

While mentors are typically not your boss at work, that is how I met and came to mentor the author. Tonya stood out because she set high standards for herself and was not afraid to seek, and apply, feedback to strengthen and improve her knowledge and skills. Good bosses promote their people to others and help them take advantage of growth opportunities elsewhere in the company so it was as rewarding for me, as it was for her, when Tonya was promoted, left my department where she had been in a key training and development role, and moved to a new HR position. Over the years, we have maintained our connection and Tonya continues to reach out for informal conversations and more formal mentoring advice such as when she was debating whether to pursue an MBA degree while working full-time. It is a privilege to be contacted by Tonya as I always learn something from our conversations too!

Remember that coaches and mentors, like friends, will be in your life for a reason, for a season, or for a lifetime. Whether you seek them out or they fall into your life - make the most of your time with them. It can be life changing.

Now you have some insight as to why Nancy has been the consummate Mentor to me for all these years, and I wouldn't have it any other way. Thank you, Nancy. You've made my life richer with your sage advice, and ever ready friendship, even when years pass between contact.

Now let's explore how you can leverage the knowledge gained from this chapter to engage a coach, mentor, or seek support from others to pursue your goals.

#LIFESUPPORT

ACTIVITY PAGE

If you have a Coach(es) or Mentor(s), please list. If not, identify who you would like to be your Coach or Mentor.

_____

_____

_____

_____

_____

_____

_____

_____

Why have you chosen the above to be your Coach(es)/Mentor(s).

_____

_____

_____

_____

_____

_____

_____

_____

_____

_____

APPLICATION

If you have a Coach(es)/Mentor(s), plan what you'd like to discuss for your next meeting in alignment with this chapter. If not, plan how you would like to request for the ones that you are interested in becoming your Coach(es)/Mentor(s).

_____

_____

_____

_____

_____

_____

_____

_____

_____

_____

_____

_____

_____

_____

_____

_____

_____

_____

_____

CHAPTER 8

Emotions Aren't Bad (EQ & Building Relationships)

e·mo·tion·al in·tel·li·gence
/əˈmōSH(ə)n(ə)l/ /inˈteləjəns/

the ability to recognize and understand
emotions, and use this awareness to manage
yourself and your relationship with others

Because we can't live life alone without going a little crazy, it's important to connect with people in an effective manner to get things done. The brain works in such a way that we feel things first. When something happens to us (a stimulus), it travels up our spinal cord to the back of our brains to the limbic system where our emotions reside. As we recognize and understand the emotions that we are feeling, the front side of the brain, the rational side, helps to decide what to do with the emotions and potentially how to manage it. To illustrate this concept, you see a small puppy chasing after a ball that is almost as big as she is. You probably experience a feeling of happiness, and then you smile, and you may even want to pick up the puppy for a hug. However, let's say you are allergic to dogs. In this case, your awareness of the situation -- how you want to pick up the puppy, but also noting that you picking up the puppy may make you sick as a result – will cause you to think about whether to avoid picking up the cute little puppy or not. How you think about a situation affects your behavior. You can also apply this cause and effect approach to become more proactive in how you deal with your emotions instead of only reacting to them. You can have more control over the outcome of interactions with others.

The topic of this chapter is based on the book Emotional Intelligence 2.0 written by Travis Bradberry and Jean Greaves. This book offers ways to increase Emotional Intelligence (EQ).

The reason that this is so important is that studies show across industries that top performers tend to have a high EQ (see statistics below). Over 42,000 people had their EQ tested, and then researchers compared their salaries, resulting in a higher salary for those who were more emotionally intelligent. That isn't to say that intelligence isn't important too, but IQ is established at an early age, whereas EQ continues to grow when practiced regularly.

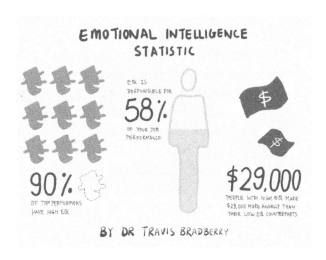

EMOTIONAL INTELLIGENCE STATISTIC

EQ IS RESPONSIBLE FOR 58% OF YOUR JOB PERFORMANCE

90% OF TOP PERFORMERS HAVE HIGH EQ

$29,000 PEOPLE WITH HIGH EQ MAKE $29,000 MORE ANNUALLY THAN THEIR LOW EQ COUNTERPARTS

BY DR TRAVIS BRADBERRY

Having had the opportunity to become certified as an Emotional Intelligence Facilitator, I have experienced the effect of gaining additional knowledge on the subject, applying it myself, and mentoring others to do the same. It has had a profound impact on not only my relationship with others, but also with other areas of my life because it is a mindful, cognitive approach to making changes that may be needed in life. For me, in addition to relationship building, this approach has led to weight loss, better stress management, maintaining a healthier lifestyle, and more. With this approach, you may also be able to experience success in areas for which you'd like growth.

So, if reacting to your emotions without a filter is something that you struggle with, this chapter might be beneficial for you. It speaks to a level of personal and social competence where awareness of both can lead to the better management of a set of related core skills. The indication is that what you see in yourself (self-awareness) will allow you to choose what to do about what you discover (self-management), but also what you see in others (social awareness) will allow you to choose what to do with what you discover (relationship management). Successfully navigating these core skills can ultimately result in improved communications and relationships with others.

My focus for the reader in this chapter is more about personal competence because this book is specifically about addressing and planning for your personal leadership journey. Becoming more self-aware and choosing how to self-manage to consistently achieve positive outcomes is an important part of doing so. What's especially important to remember is that **EMOTIONS AREN'T BAD!** They are a natural and normal response to all situations. But you can practice control over them, so they don't overtake you or the situation. The best way to describe how this happens is through the Trigger Model, taught by TalentSmart, which explains how emotions affect our actions.

Basically, what happens is that an event occurs to trigger an emotional reaction in you. Now if you act without thinking, especially if your emotional response is strong, such as anger, the results could be negative. However, you can assert control over this by recognizing the emotion you're feeling as quickly as possible. It may even be a common emotional response to a certain event, like being cut off in traffic on the highway at 65 MPH or seeing an individual with whom you've had conflicts in the past. Because you know this in advance, you can stop, breathe, hesitate, talk to yourself, and decide to act differently. You do this by not ignoring how you feel, accepting and acknowledging the emotion, taking a breath so that you slow down to buy yourself some time to respond, talking yourself through several positive options, and then from there deciding to act differently from the choice of positive courses of action you were considering. Although this does not guarantee a positive outcome, you are more likely to do so.

This process allows you to manage your emotions more mindfully and in ways that are more beneficial to you and others. The following is a real-life example of how beneficial this approach can be as Chris M. shares how EQ helped him grow as a leader in the performing arts. He was originally involved in several sports with the hopes of earning a scholarship to college. However, Chris decided late in high school that he was interested in the theater and performing arts (More of Chris's story to be shared in Chapter 10, Thinking Out of the Box - Creativity.). He enjoyed taking on the persona of different characters, pretending not to be himself. He had a natural instinct for it. It required him to tap into his feelings and the feelings of the characters he played to delve deeper and understand why the character feels that way. At one theatrical workshop, he played a bully. He tried to put himself in the shoes of his character, and his level of empathy allowed him to see that the bully felt worthless, and angry with himself for having feelings for the young man that he was bullying. He played the character this way, and it resonated with another workshop participant who was dealing with something similar in her life. A true form of art imitating life; the perfect trifecta connection of understanding yourself, understanding the character, and merging the two to realistically portray the results. Chris was able to recognize and understand the emotions both in himself and others and interpret those feelings in his acting in such a way that it helped someone else. *"This"*, he said, *"is why I love what I do!"*

When considering how to affect a positive outcome or to help others in different situations, you tend to look more outside of yourself. This is a key step toward being more socially aware. To do this effectively, you should practice actively listening to what others say, and how they say it; watching others' behaviors, and their body language; and asking questions to get the whole picture or story before engaging. That's what Chris did when researching his character. When you do so, you'll best be able to understand your needs and the needs of others as you seek to achieve what is required together. Together we can accomplish so much more than working alone. When done purposefully and mindfully, you can build wonderful relationships and partnerships.

But, here's another perspective. Paula Green is the former Vice President of Learning & Development at my company. She was instrumental in the introduction of Mastering Emotional Intelligence as a strategic initiative to our organization in 2016. The feedback from the beginning of that journey has been that this was a valuable investment for the company. As a colleague and friend, her insights on EQ can also be valuable to you.

Tonya has talked about how building emotional intelligence skills can change your life. And I would add that they can also prepare you for life. They have certainly added a depth of understanding and purpose to mine. And for that change and understanding to happen you need to be able to:

- **Understand Who You are Now and Who You Want to Be**

- **Build Emotional Intelligence Skills You Can Use in Every Facet of Your Life – Personal Life, School Life, and Work Life**

- **Manage Interactions with Others to Realize the Best Outcomes**

- **Improve Your Connections and Relationships**

Understand Who You are Now, and Who You Want to Be

I recently met with a group of young women and they described themselves in a variety of ways:

- I'm nice or kind

- I'm a perfectionist

- I'm a pleaser

- I want to accomplish everything on my own

- I'm confident/I'm not confident

- I like to control everything

- I speak my mind

- I'm not comfortable asking for help

Do one or more of these statements resonate with you? If not, add a description of yourself to the list.

When I asked about how they were managing or working on the challenges they faced, they talked about the following:

- I'm trying not to control everything
- I'm working on remaining calm and not letting others affect me
- I'm leaning more on myself to get through tough situations
- I'm growing in confidence and standing up for myself
- I'm learning I can't be everything to everybody - I'm finding balance
- I'm saying "no" and it's liberating
- I'm taking ownership of my own life
- I'm communicating how I feel to others
- I'm being more honest
- I'm taking responsibility for my actions

Building emotional intelligence starts with your answers to these two questions.

In understanding yourself, right now:

1. What do you do well?
2. What do you want to improve? Or what would you like to do more of or less of?

Being aware of your own emotions and how your emotions can affect others, once you understand that, you can work on skills that were talked about earlier in this chapter to begin managing your emotions to a better emotional outcome for yourself and for your relationships with others.

The balance of this chapter is focused on thoughts and tips that may be helpful to you as you begin to think about your personal journey to build your emotional intelligence.

Build Emotional Intelligence Skills You Can Use in Every Facet of Your Life – Personal Life, School Life, and Work Life

- Identify the area(s) you want to work on and the possible solutions you will try. Then think about what will motivate you to make the change. How important is what you want to work on to you? What will be different when you've made the change? Then write down your goal(s) and the strategies and tactics you want to try.

- In order to change how you've approached certain people or situations over the course of your life and to install emotional intelligence skill sets, you will need to practice…practice...and then practice some more. How you initially react to people and situations could be a pretty deep-seated habit. It will take your continued effort to affect the changes you want to make. And it will take time for the new skills and behaviors you're practicing becoming second nature to you.

- Possessing emotional intelligence also assists you in building good "soft skills". Soft skills are your personal character traits that enable you to interact effectively with other people. You might also call them interpersonal skills. These skills can enhance your time management, effective communication, problem-solving ability, stress tolerance, flexibility, and teamwork. Throughout your entire life, soft skills will always be your most valuable asset.

- And there is something I would like all young women to remember. And that's to get into the habit of **taking credit for the work you've successfully accomplished**. Many times, women give credit, for the most part, to others and don't communicate well what they've achieved. You need to earn respect…. but don't undervalue your work. So, be honest and give credit where credit is due……just don't forget about yourself when you do.

Manage Interactions with Others to Achieve the Best Outcomes

-In each situation you face with a person or a group, ask yourself - How do I feel? What would be the best outcome for this particular situation? What's my objective? You might also ask yourself – How does the person or group you're interacting with feel? And when you've finished the discussion or closed an issue ask yourself – Would I have done anything differently? What did I learn? Analyzing your outcome can be extremely valuable in your continued ability to hone and fine tune your skills. Remember, what you identified that you would like to do better next time is an opportunity for development and improvement.

-Important information to keep in mind during any personal interaction:

- Limit distractions. This can be hard to do, but so important in making a connection with others. Life is full of interruptions and your many devices can make it extremely difficult to stay in the moment. I urge you to be present and focused. Some things that help are a) limit multi-tasking; and b) use your computer camera, FaceTime, and Zoom. If you can be seen, you are more likely to be and stay engaged.

- Keep calm and collected. Think through the situation, ask questions to understand, keep your emotions in check and respond clearly and with respect to the other person or group.

- Watch your body language. A large part of communication is non-verbal. Make sure that your expressions and body language match what you are saying.

- Make good eye contact. When you do, you show a level of respect for and connection to the person or group you are speaking with.

- Don't forget to breathe. Taking a calming breath releases tension which will help you to think and stay focused on the positive outcome you're looking for.

- Avoid talking over or interrupting people. Waiting until they're finished speaking shows that you are attentive and thoughtful.

- Seek out diversity of thought. Look for people whose opinions are different from your own. Strive to understand their positions. What can you learn from their background? You may need to show your vulnerability and share your story with them. Then you can ask about their story. If you come from a place of openness, you will set a foundation for inclusivity and be better prepared to learn, connect and bridge any divide. Then you will be on the road to building long term, lasting relationships of trust.

Improve Your Connections and Relationships

So how do you take what you know about yourself and others and build strong, resilient relationships?

- Make sure you have a complete picture of what is going on. Not just what's easy to see on the exterior but ask questions until you can see the whole picture. Don't make assumptions…know for sure. Can you alter the quality of your listening skills? "Active" listening should allow you to keep engaged on the thoughts and observations of the other person or group of people instead of on what you want to ask next.

- Ask others for their opinions of your strengths and areas you can work on. And resist being defensive about what others may tell you. Stay open and learn from others. Their feedback is a gift. And then, as I mentioned before, build a small group of people who you trust to help mentor or coach you with your emotional intelligence skills. Ask for their opinion or request their assistance in role playing with you through challenges you are having with either a situation, individual or group of people.

- "The Power of Positive Thinking" – Norman Vincent Peale had it right. Having a positive attitude can make a tremendous difference in how you manage your emotional intelligence and in how you will build your skills over time. Set a plan for how you want to leverage not only your emotional strengths, but what you will do to make adjustments or corrections to behaviors you want to improve. And you must view any missteps or setbacks as opportunities to grow. Think positive. Make an adjustment in your tactics or try something new and then try again. There will be many opportunities to utilize your skills because you can practice them across your personal, school and work life.

In Conclusion

In thinking back to the discussion that I had with the group of young women I mentioned before, one of them said a comment said to her a few years ago had made such a difference in her life. She had made a hard decision, and after making it, she began to worry over and question her decision. The person she was talking to her said this – "Do the best you can with the knowledge you have at the time." What great advice. You will not show perfect emotional intelligence every day of your life because each day you are learning about the world around you. Understand who you are, what you believe and how you will articulate your beliefs. As I mentioned earlier, you are on your personal life journey. And along your path, keep developing - uncover what's important to you, how you want to live your life and care for others, with the ultimate goal to identify and build a life and career that is meaningful to you.

So, be an observer of people. Be curious. But also see yourself clearly and be totally involved in building your one life. Know that when you are seen as an empathetic, caring and responsible person, when you take initiative and are seen as a problem solver or trusted advisor, you will be building life and leadership skills that will be visible to everyone in your personal, community and work life.

Here's to your life and to your journey. Take good care of it.

Wise words from a wonderful EQ practitioner. Now let's apply what you've learned in the next activities.

#BEYONDIQ

ACTIVITY PAGE

Identify multiple relationships where you can practice your EQ skills and list them below.

_____

_____

_____

_____

_____

_____

_____

_____

Analyze each of these relationships by noting what your needs are, their needs, and what's of you required together? It's important to put yourself in their shoes; however, if you don't know, ask.

_____

_____

_____

_____

_____

_____

_____

_____

_____

APPLICATION

Think about your best friend or the most important person in your life. Why do they have that special distinction? What emotional skills do they possess? Write their strengths down and think about which of their skills you would like to learn to improve yourself.

_____

_____

_____

_____

_____

_____

_____

_____

_____

_____

_____

_____

_____

_____

_____

_____

_____

_____

CHAPTER 9

Think Out of the Box (Be Creative)

cre·a·tiv·i·ty
/ˌkrēāˈtivədē/

using one's imagination, original ideas, and
innovations to develop the new

One common topic that came up in the survey was the concern that there are times when there aren't clear options to practice leadership roles during these formative years between 13 and 18, or that the options are limited. The lack of opportunities emphasized the need for a chapter like this. What it offers are insights on how some have been able to overcome this obstacle. It becomes necessary to be a bit creative in these situations.

I'd like to first start with James B.'s story.

James has always aimed to be in leadership positions throughout high school. There, he was the President of multiple organizations: one of which was created by his friend that catered specifically to Black students, an area of interest for James, and another was an organization focus on career development. James created a handful of events but did not accomplish his goals alone because he knew the power of a question. He wanted to create a community service event, so he asked school officials, organization members, and friends to support a school-wide clothing drive for the homeless in the community. The response was extremely generous. Creating, developing, and implementing that event allowed him to lead, not by title, but because anyone willing to create a new activity or venture and ask for help to coordinate it has then made their own leadership role.

When James graduated from high school and went to college, as an incoming Freshman, he saw the opportunity to lead as a blank slate. James wanted to place himself in new leadership roles, so he applied for and got accepted to be a marketing chair for his school's Black Student Alliance and a chair of an organization catering to mentorship in the Black community. He became more invested in social activism and was motivated to create a new space and opportunity for Black students to celebrate their culture, so he founded a stomp and shake team that he named 'Lights Out'. He'd never created a program this large before, but the mission of the organization motivated him to keep going and see it through. He used the same principles from high school — he planned on his own, then he asked school officials and friends for support. Because there were limited options for creative spaces and leadership roles for Black students, James found his way to leadership by creating a new one.

James' approach isn't new, but the outcome was a new organization. This is a direction that you can take if there is a lack of opportunities available to you, or if what is available is not of interest to you.

There are many more creative ways to practice leadership skills. Another one that comes to mind is especially fun and offers great experiential learning. It's a Leadership Reaction Course for youth. Teams of youth navigate outdoor obstacles, where they climb, crawl, scoot, lift, swing, and more. Each participant get to take a turn as the leader. These Leader Reaction Courses are often part of youth leadership camps, where participants learn from each assigned task about their leadership abilities, strengths, communication skills, and how to develop as individual leaders.

You've read of a couple of ways to creatively practice leading. Here's another story that shows some additional insight on not just looking at the traditional opportunities that are available.

Returning to Christopher M., he took an unorthodox route to becoming a performance artist. Honestly, he was encouraged to choose a different route. He played basketball, football, and took martial arts, and was successful in all three. The initial path was to be considered for a sports scholarship to attend college. However, these activities started to take a toll on him physically. Even though this seemed the best route to enter college, he wanted to consider other options.

Chris enjoyed singing in the choir at church, and later became involved in the drama and mime ministries too. What started as a hobby, turned into an area of focus. He not only participated as a performing artist at church but joined a theater training class in high school to learn the basics and the lingo of the theater. This was typically a freshman class, but he took it as a senior since his interest had been sparked. He'd always appreciated movies, and he liked the idea of stepping outside of himself to become other characters, so it wasn't a stretch to from a spectator to a performer. He enjoyed it so much that he decided that he wanted to give it a shot to study in college, and ultimately make it his career. Since then, he has written, directed, choreographed, and performed in various artistic endeavors, received accolades and scholarships from his efforts, and his future looks bright even though the start was anything but typical.

As in many of the offered examples throughout this book, you have and will see where others started their leadership journey as the member of a sports team. This is probably one of the most popular ways of doing so. However, not everyone is athletic, and even if you are, everyone doesn't always make the team. So, identifying all the different organization leadership options is another way to creatively find what will work best for you. What you may find is an important, but less traveled path. This brings to mind that several of the survey takers, especially the Traditionalists and Baby Boomer generations fondly remembered their experiences leading within the Girl scouts. The fact that it wasn't a costly option made it more accessible to girls. As Sheila T. remarked, "We did not extend ourselves. We did not have the money to do activities, and that was a barrier. However,

Girl Scouts did not require a lot of funding, so I found my place there."

Several Traditionalists, Baby Boomers, and Generation X survey takers were Girl Scouts and shared the importance of that activities where they learned about leadership and practice demonstrating those skills along with how to support others by being a good friend. The Girl Scouts promotes much of what is shared in this book. It teaches ways to be positive, supportive, and show a good attitude. Their Scout slogan is about being kind on a large and small scale. They promise to serve and help others. And the Girl Scout Law professes that each ". . . will do my best to be honest and fair, friendly and helpful, considerate and caring, courageous and strong, and responsible for what I say and do, and to respect myself and others, respect authority, use resources wisely, make the world a better place, and be a sister to every Girl Scout." This commitment mirrors what we see in some of the best leaders today. Although the Girl Scouts is not as popular as it once was, both it and the Boy Scouts are a creative but less common route to practice leadership skills. As a matter of fact, the Boy Scouts is open to girls. So, if you prefer outdoor activities, this may be another way for you to practice leadership through an avenue that is of interest to you.

Next, I'd like to try something a little different. Creativity is not my strong suit, and I've been known to leverage innovative ideas when considering a different approach to a solution. I admire those who can create completely original ideas and art. You've seen the creative artwork of Todd Sprow as the illustrator for each chapter, but as we conclude this chapter, I would like to showcase the creativity and artistic skills of him and a few others.

The purpose of this exercise is to look at a subject differently than you normally would. Instead of reading and journaling about your experiences, I want you to find a solution in a completely different manner. In this exercise, you're going to flex your creative brain over your analytical one.

These artistic creations represent the journey of their creators through some of the chapter topics that you've read so far. See if you can determine which chapters are represented in each piece of art. Some may represent multiple chapters.

#OUTSIDETHEBOX

Printed card by Todd, the illustrator's artwork from 10 years ago, when I first considered writing this book, and two more recent pieces.

Rendering by Melzario. The General Motors Design Center outreach program exposed high schoolers in Detroit to considering vehicle design as a career and art school for college. Melzario was one of those students.

When I look in the mirror I see change.
When I look at my parents, King and Queen.
I was made in Your image So I'm the same.
I can't be scared.
My only limit is me.
My Daddy said, "Son, don't worry. It's just pain."
My Mama told me, "Don't worry. You just pray."
Any moment That's pressuring my faith,
Go to the Father in Heaven And just say…
Can I walk with You today? I've got a couple questions for You.
Can I talk with You today? I've got a couple questions for You.

Lyrics for 'Yes You Can' by Baby Brother

Sketches by Hillary, who turned to art when struggling with depression & social anxiety.

Art by Faith, who is exploring her passion.

Some Other Time	**Let Me Introduce Myself (re-visioning "Some Other Time")**
no, I wasn't sleeping just in deep thought sometimes I can get lost doing this	No, I wasn't sleeping... just in deep thought Sometimes, I can get lost doing this
...thinking about this or that sometimes regressing to where I've been or pretending to be somewhere I'm not or even someone else...	thinking and pondering about this or that... sometimes regressing to where I've been other times just thinking about where I'd rather be most times...
someone stronger **than i** tougher than **ME**	I am simply preparing to propel... to catapult myself
someone like let's see	in a whole new direction with a purposed intention there is no one tougher than I no one... stronger
a Black Superwoman	I.. I am Superwoman
yeah you too...?	you too...
I thought I was the only one	I ain't surprised

Poetry by Kitra on her journey to self-discovery

Art by William, the second is part of a series to raise funds for the homeless.

Art by Kate, protégé of the illustrator.

CHAPTER 10

Keep Your Eye on the Prize (Focus & Positive Outlook)

fo·cus
/ˈfōkəs/

clear direction and center of attention

pos·i·tiv·i·ty
/ˌpäzəˈtivədē/

the tendency to have an optimistic
or 'can do' attitude

I've always believed that synergy comes from including the dynamics of different perspectives within a team of decision makers. The process may take longer, but the result considers different concerns where the outcome won't be the result of "group think" where everyone agrees with each other without question, or just goes along to get along. Having optimists, pessimists, and realists deciding together can be challenging, but the contributions will make for a richer solution. The optimist tends to have the philosophy that ultimately, good will prevail. The pessimist tends to believe that the worst will happen. The realist tends to remain in the present, focused on the current facts and observations. When combined and each, no matter his/her perspective, has a 'can do' attitude, meaning that they believe that a resolution can be reached that will meet the overall needs, this is where synergy happens. The decision makers must be willing and open-minded enough to hear other opinions to reach that solution together.

This is my perspective when I think of teams, but everyone has a responsibility to contribute to that 'can do' attitude. If you remember the insight of Dr. Jones in Chapter 3, Know Stuff (Continuous Learning), she shared some observations of different personalities working together to achieve a common goal in the Marshmallow Challenge. Those who participated were engaged and contributed to the results of building the tallest structure out of the given materials in 18 minutes. I'm sure that you can imagine the energy level in an activity like that with all the numerous opinions, frustrations with falling structures, and elation for accomplishing the goal and maybe even winning. However, the outcome can be so rewarding to each team member because teamwork does matter and tends to offer the best results when everyone is focused on achieving a positive outcome.

Here are some examples of how individuals remained focused, with a positive outlook, even in the face of adversity.

Lori T. shared the following:

I dreamed of going to a Military Service Academy and I was determined to make it! I was driven because it would allow me to achieve my goals of becoming an Engineer and give me the scholarship I needed to attend a quality college. The more I researched Service Academies, the more I believed that this was the best route for me. So, between my Junior and Senior year of high school, I talked my family into renting an RV and taking a "vacation" to visit each Service Academy..

First we went to the Merchant Marine Academy and on the tour, I asked about the academic Majors available. The guide said, "We have two types of Majors - above deck and below deck." I wanted to be an Engineer, but that was a little too tight for me. So, I said, "Thank you. I'll be on my way".

Next, we went to the Coast Guard Academy. I really like water so I could see myself on a boat. During the tour, the guide said, "We only accept people based on academic merit." Since I was more well-rounded and knew that this was not my primary strength, again I said, "Thank you. I'll be on my way."

Then we visited the Naval Academy. I'm a strong swimmer, so maybe this was the right academy for me. However, I wasn't met with a warm reception. Actually, I felt unwelcome. So, for the third time, I said, "Thank you. I'll be on my way."

Our final stop was at the United States Military Academy in West Point, New York. We drove on to the Post and stopped just inside the gate at Buffalo Soldiers Field. I threw my hands in the air and said, "This is it! This is where I'm going to go to college!" The tour only solidified this. So, when I returned home. I contacted my Congressman with my interest and that set things in motion for my attending West Point.

What is clear in this example is not only her focus, but to ensure that she maintained a positive outlook, in the end, she needed to find a place where she fit and felt welcome. This is critical to success.

Focus also requires establishing boundaries. It's hard to move forward without creating boundaries around the things that can impede your progress. Sometimes this may require eliminating the distraction or limiting it.

Caleb C. is an excellent example of limiting distractions toward achieving his goal of becoming a body builder. At 12, he was taller than many kids, but lanky. However, he was handsome, danced well, and had swagger (for however much you can have it in middle school), so it didn't bother him. Then he went to high school and had more competition. He wrestled in league competition and was pretty good at it, but decided he preferred Track & Field. He started to bulk up and get stronger but was looking more thick and solid than muscular. Part of this is because he loves sweets. However, he became determined to define his muscles more. As the definition started to show, he liked what he saw, and decided that one day he would like to perform in a body building competition. This meant exercising his will over his love of sweets, as well as spending many hours in the gym. The latter was easy. The gym and training became his passion to the point that he got his certification and began to train others. Sweets on the other hand were still his weakness.

Since he knew he would have a difficult time eliminating them completely from his diet, he built in a reward system for accomplishments.

For instance: If I gain this level of definition, I can have cookies, or if I get to this weight, I can have a candy bar. This more "delayed gratification" plan worked!

His focus, and approach to managing his love of sweets allowed him to reach his goal of performing in a body building competition. Although he came in second place out of 10 competitors, the competition was remarkably close.

Another part of focus is practicing patience. We live in a microwave generation and can immediately view events that occur around the world through social media. The adage *Patience is a virtue*, doesn't seem to be valued as much as it used to. However, recognizing when patience is needed and practicing it can lead to tremendous outcomes.

As an example, let's return to Caleb's story. The previous example shows that he decided at 16 that he wanted to become a body builder. Clearly, this doesn't happen overnight. His steady commitment and patience not to give up when the going was tough allowed him to achieve this one goal FIVE YEARS LATER! Now that is patience and a single-minded focus.

Let's apply some of what you've learned from this chapter in the following exercises.

#FOCUSDON'TSPRAY

ACTIVITY PAGE

What distraction often prevents you from progressing forward? How do you plan to establish boundaries to eliminate or minimize the impact of the distraction?

_____

_____

_____

_____

_____

_____

_____

When working with a team, how do you go about making sure that your voice is heard and that you listen to others? How do you determine when to compromise?

_____

_____

_____

_____

_____

_____

_____

_____

_____

APPLICATION

At one of your next meetings, when a decision is being made, try to take a perspective that is completely different from your own (e.g. If you tend to be pessimistic, try an optimistic perspective to find a solution.)

_____

_____

_____

_____

_____

_____

_____

_____

_____

_____

_____

_____

_____

_____

_____

_____

_____

_____

_____

CHAPTER 11

Stuff Happens
(Expect Setbacks)

setbacks
/ˈsetbacks/

an interruption to progress

Imagine that life is moving along in the direction that you expect. All your plans are coming to fruition. Things are falling into place very nicely. Then WHAM! Out of the blue, your ideal plans are ruined! How did this happen? You planned everything perfectly!

Unfortunately, or fortunately, life is not ideal. Stuff happens that takes you off the path that you were on, and potentially prepares you for or creates a better path that you may not have thought of without the setback. Not only that, character is built and can be strengthened when dealing with setbacks based on how you deal with them.

For better understanding of what I mean, this is what happened to me. I was working part-time in a role as the leader of a company. After completing a year in this role, I was assigned to a staff position. My first weekend of training with them was in October. During the weekend training, we were scheduled to complete a fitness test. I was more than ready, but the weather wasn't accommodating. It had significantly rained the previous day, then the temperature dropped to below freezing overnight. What we were not aware of was that the trails we were planning to use for the running portion of the fitness test had also been used for motor-cross bike racing the previous day, so the ground froze with ruts on the route. While running on the uneven ground, I tripped and was about to fall, but was able to catch myself and stand upright before toppling over. Unfortunately, when I did that, I heard or felt something pop in my back. I kept running, trying to gauge how I felt, but I just felt numb from the cold, so I thought I was fine.

We were released after that event, and I started to drive home. As my body started to warm up, I started to feel painful twinges in my back, legs, and neck. Over the next three days, it got so bad that I could barely walk. I went to the doctor, and after an MRI, it was discovered that I had two bulging discs in my upper back where I'd felt the original pop. I reported it to my boss but continued to work and seek treatments to help minimize or alleviate the pain.

Fast forward six months later, and I was up for promotion for my next assignment, which would have been an international one. As we prepared for travel, the doctor reviewed my MRI and told me that I would not be able to go on the assignment because my injury was too serious. My body would not be able to handle the physical requirements to do the job.

So, I had to remain state-side until the business unit returned. However, when they did return, I received a letter that said that my services were no longer needed. I was being released from my responsibilities for medical reasons. I was shocked! I'd always been a top performer. My mind was still intact, and I still wanted to work. Another local business unit had even requested that they wanted me to transfer to them, but to no avail. Instead, this part of my career was over, and not on my own terms.

Needless to say, I was extremely disappointed. That is probably the understatement of the decade! Thinking about it still hurts. My family tried to cheer me up with letters of encouragement, hugs, and kisses. Each of them frequently expressed the importance of my being home with them versus being on an international assignment. However, I couldn't shake how hurt I felt. This was truly a setback from my original plans of this part-time gig becoming more. Then one day, about a month after this happened, I was given the opportunity by my full-time company to go back to school for my master's degree in my field of choice, HR, and they were paying for it! If I had been able to go on the international assignment, I would not have been able to take advantage of this wonderful opportunity, and I may not be where I am today, doing what I love! The setback set me up for a better plan than I could have even dreamed for myself.

Don't believe me? Here's another example.

Lynn T. had a major setback in High School. During a soccer game in her Junior year of high school, the night before Prom, she slipped on the field and went down hard. She knew immediately that this was serious. A visit to the doctor confirmed this. She'd torn ligaments in her right knee. Soccer was not over for just the season, but completely. The next evening for Prom, she didn't sit home and mope. Instead, she had a wonderful time at Prom, even if at times from a wheelchair or dancing using crutches. After final exams, she had surgery and had to keep her leg straight for six weeks, with a special brace.

But this was only the first setback. She also played tennis on the Junior Varsity team. Although new to the sport, she was positive, supportive, and encouraging with the Freshmen and Sophomore girls. Tennis was no longer an option either. Needless to say, she was very disappointed.

When asked her how she got through this trial, she said simply, *"Physical therapy, A lot of crying, Surgery, and a strong desire to walk and run again. I had to do the work. No one could do it for me."* Not only did she come through this stronger, but now when other young ladies go through hard times, she is helpful in reminding them that trials will come, but they will get through whatever they are, and as a result, become stronger and more resilient. For this, she is thankful.

Alright, just one more. Are you with me? Hang with me here!

Elizabeth T. had played travel soccer for several years. When trying out for the Upper Teams in high school with all her friends, an extra day of tryout was scheduled at the last minute in order for the new Coach to watch everyone for the first time. However, she had a conflict with a choir concert for which she was singing and missed it. She found out that week that he didn't make the team. This was devastating and frustrating to her because she was the leading scorer and the fastest girl on the team according to the stats, and these were the friends she'd played soccer with for years. She tried to speak with the Coach about a make-up tryout date, but all that was offered was a spot to be a leader on the Lower Level Team to earn her way back to the Upper Level Team. This felt like a demotion because she felt like she'd already earned a spot on the Upper Level Team. She and her family knew that this move would instead very demotivating and this would not bring out the best in her. Her self-esteem, pride and self-worth would not allow this as an option.

Instead, since this was the local town team, she and her family contacted the best travel league in the city. Hey, why not? They immediately gave her a tryout ad she ended up on a travel team that was two levels above the Upper Team! She moved over and up and had an excellent soccer season. She would not have this experience if she had not had the initial setback. She would have never chosen to leave the local town team, but instead ended up playing in a bigger league on a better Upper Level team.

You get my point. I'm sure you can share a few stories of your own. These examples remind me of the phrase "We cannot control the wind, but we can adjust the sails." It speaks of focusing on what we can control and influence. It doesn't mean that we won't be impacted by outside factors, but it refers to what we choose to do about them that builds our character and lifts us higher than our circumstances. Find the "silver lining" and move forward. Maintain the mantra that, "It's gonna be OK!" because **THAT** is the truth.

The next set of activities is about recognizing that setbacks are temporary and identifying what you've learned from them.

#SETUPFORBETTER

ACTIVITY PAGE

Note a recent setback? How did it make you feel?

_____

_____

_____

_____

_____

_____

_____

_____

_____

What could you control or influence that may have contributed to the setback? Reflect on lessons learned.

_____

_____

_____

_____

_____

_____

_____

_____

_____

_____

<u>APPLICATION</u>

You are given the opportunity to go back in time to coach yourself through this setback. What would that conversation sound like?

_____

_____

_____

_____

_____

_____

_____

_____

_____

_____

_____

_____

_____

_____

_____

_____

_____

_____

_____

_____

CHAPTER 12

What's Next?
(Goals & Milestones)

goals
/gōlz/

primary aims or desired results

Now that you've received some of what I believe to be foundational information to get started on your leadership journey, you may be asking, *"What do I do now?"*

My suggestion is to define what is most important to you, then be **SMART** in your approach of setting up goals to achieve your objective(s). **SMART** stands for **S**pecific, **M**easurable, **A**ppropriate, **R**esults-Oriented, and **T**ime-Based. Others have also used Attainable or Achievable for the **A**, but Appropriate speaks to areas for which the individual has some control.

SMART is a key guideline in writing impactful goals which clearly identify your intended direction, and defines what success looks like. This way, you can focus your efforts, and improve your chances of achieving a successful outcome. Let's define each one individually:

Specific   Precisely describe the out-
                  come that you want.

Measurable   Identify a reliable method
                  to measure progress toward
                  achievement of the goal.

Appropriate   Choose something meaning-
                  ful and something over which
                  you have control.

Results-Oriented The goal, if successfully
                  accomplished, helps to
                  achieve your "super why".

Time-Based   Clearly define when you plan
                  to start/finish this goal.

Goal alignment with your "super why" is very important. When you are distracted from the goal, reminding yourself of the core reason why achieving the goal is so important to you so that you can keep you on track, or bring you back on track.

Here's an example:

Achieve an A- or above in AP History by the end of the semester to get on the Principal's Honor Roll.

Does it meet the SMART criteria? It's specifically speaking to one particular class. The grade desired is the measurement method. It's appropriate because good grades are meaningful to me. Getting on the Principal's Honor Roll will be the result by the end of the semester, which is the timeframe.

Then check to see if the goal aligns with your "super why". Let's say it's to be academically ready to get into a college of your choice with a merit scholarship to prevent or minimize your parents from paying for your education. Yep! There's alignment! See, that wasn't so bad!

Keep in mind that goals may take a while to achieve, so to stay on track, identify some interim milestones to make sure that you are making progress. An example might be getting a certain grade on your mid-term exam to remain on track to receive the overall grade that you want by the end of the semester. It is also helpful to have an accountability partner (a friend, coach, mentor, etc.); someone who will help you stay focused on the end goal, and assist with checking progress, giving you honest feedback along the way, or suggesting ways to get back on track if there has been a distraction, disruption, or setback.

When setting goals and milestones for yourself, think about the purpose. What are your core values in life? Focus on what you do well. Think about what you enjoy. Understand why a certain skillset is a strength for you. Then create goals that stay in alignment with those values through your behaviors, thoughts, and actions. When you understand where you're starting from, and where you'd like to go, it's easier to write SMART goals."

My final suggestion is to be patient and flexible. Long term change or the best outcomes aren't easily rushed. Also, your priorities may change. You're young, so you may discover new areas of interest, or setbacks may occur to change your focus. Theodore Roosevelt once said, "Do what you can, with what you have, where you are." So just, modify your SMART goal with the new information and priorities. Laurel T. indicated, "The most beneficial thing to my wellbeing when my injury prevented me from playing soccer was finding a new activity to be involved with, creating a shift in my priorities and goals going forward." This is okay. You will continue to adjust as you find your way, so don't be too rigid with you plans. Give yourself room to explore your options, and don't feel bad because it didn't turn out exactly as you planned.

So, there you have it. Nuggets to start your leadership journey. Ultimately, even if the entire content of this book does not resonate with you, hopefully a chapter or two inspires you to reach your highest potential. The intent is to share some foundational and fundamental leadership principles with you through examples and stories that are applicable to you and offer ways to practice and apply them to reinforce them. If I do that for one person who ends up achieving their goals because some portion of the content sparked a positive change or focus, then I have done my job.

#SMARTer

FINAL APPLICATION

Create a goal for an area where you have aspirations. Is it SMART? Check each box to the right upon comparison to the definitions offered in this chapter. Use the space below the table to jot notes to help write a clear goal on the table, and any other goals that you may have in mind. It might be helpful to write your "super why" first (the most important purpose to you).

S		☐
M		☐
A		☐
R		☐
T		☐

_____

_____

_____

_____

_____

_____

_____

_____

_____

References,
Acknowledgements,
& Recommended
Reading

References

Blasé, Joseph, et. al. *Democratic Principals in Action: Eight Pioneers.* Thousand Oaks: Corwin Press, Inc., 1995.

Bradberry, Travis and Jean Greaves, Patrick Lencioni. *Emotional Intelligence 2.0.* Sherman Oaks: TalentSmart, 2009

Buggy, Patrick. "Great Challenges Require Great Strength" MindfulAmbition.net, Mindful Ambition, 8 June 2020, https://mindfulambition. net/great-challenges-great-strength/

Buggy, Patrick. "You Can Choose Who You Want to Be" MindfulAmbition.net, Mindful Ambition, 31 October 2016, https://mindfulambition.net/archive/

Definitions. Dictionary.com, Dictionary.com. LLC, 2020, https://www.dictionary.com/

Eagly, A. et.al, 2003 July, *Psychological Bulletin*, *Vol 129*(4), 569-591

"Inspire the Next Generation". She Should Run, She Should Run, 2020, https://www.sheshouldrun.org/help-her-lead/

Robbins, S. P. and Coulter, M. (2007) *Management (9th ed.).* London: Prentice-Hall

"What is Your Learning Style?" TechWorld Language Solutions, TechWorld Language Solutions, 3 April 2018, http://techworldinc.com/what-is-your-learning-style/

Acknowledgements

Thankful Acknowledgement:

When I embarked on this book writing journey, there was such an overwhelming response of support, that I was greatly humbled. The input and feedback from survey respondents, peers, colleagues, mentors, and various leaders have shaped this book into what I hope to be a message that sparks not only an interest in future leadership for readers, but also offers young women some preliminary tools to practice with or for parents, teachers, mentors, etc. to expose young women to how to lead effectively while they are determining their future interests. For each story shared as examples throughout the book, I provided the first name and last initial of the contributor. Contributors of additional perspectives, art, and editing support are listed in the order that they appear in the book.

Contributors: (in order of appearance)

Erika Broadwater, National President, Executive Board of Directors and Office of the Chairman,

National Association of African Americans in Human Resources

Lori Hess Tompos, Adjunct Professor; CEO, Avail Consulting, LLC

Laurel Tompos, Statistics Guru & Young Professional

Dr. Roy Alston, Major (Retired), Dallas Police Department

Stephen Picarde, CEO and Talent Optimization Specialist, PIMidlantic

Dr. Victoria Jones, President, Northpointe Group Consulting, LLC

Nancy Bennett, Former Director, General Motors University

Paula Green, Former Vice President of Learning & Development

Amy Efaw, Published Author for young adults

Melody Smith, Military Professional, Editor for flow of content

Artistic Renditions: (in order of appearance)

Todd Sprow, Artist

Melzario Davis, Graduate of the College of Creative Studies

Baby Brother, Rapper

Hillary Nelson, Financial Analyst

Faith Martin, Student, Virginia Commonwealth University

Kitra Martindavis, Poet and Author of "a peace... for you"

William Hoertz, Artist & Owner, BJCreations

Kate O'Connor, Student, Virginia Commonwealth University

Melanie Johnson and Jenn Foster and the team at Elite Online Publishing for making the publishing process go so smoothly.

It was not my intent to leave anyone from this list. All the input and feedback I have received was of great value either to the writing process, research, or content and I greatly appreciate the support.

#BLESSEDBEYONDMEASURE

Recommended Reading List

Careers: The Graphic Guide to Planning Your Future by DK Children.

Do What You Are: Discover the Perfect Career for You Through the Secrets of Your Future, and Plan for your Dream Job by Carol Christen.

EQ Applied by Justin Bariso

Expect to Win by Carla A. Harris

I Am Beautiful. *Iambeautiful.org.* (Fosters self-esteem and develops leadership capabilities for girls and women. They have two great programs: HOPE mentoring program and GIRLS Leadership Development Program.)

Mentoring. *Mentor.org.* Organization dedicated to connecting young people with mentors.

Mindful Ambition by Patrick Buggy (Website)

Monday Morning Leadership for Women by Valerie Sokolosky

Multipliers: How the Best Leaders Make Everyone Smarter by Greg McKeown and Liz Wiseman

Perception by Brian Joyce

Personality Type by Paul D. Tieger, Barbara Barron, and Kelly Tieger.

Pink Bat: Turning Problems into Solutions by Michael McMillan

Pitch Like a Girl by Ronna Lichtenberg

The 5 Levels of Leadership by John Maxwell

The First 90 Days: Critical Success Strategies for New Leaders at All Levels by Michael Watkins

Your Why Matters Now: How Some Achieve More and Others Don't by Justin Jones-Fosu

What Color is your Parachute? For Teens, Third Edition: Discover Yourself, Design

You Got This!: Unleash Your Awesomeness, Find Your Path, and Change Your World by Maya Penn.

About the Author

Tonya Carter is from Manassas, Virginia. She grew up in a family culture of helping others and continues to draw great satisfaction from it. After high school, her family pushed her to attend the United States Military Academy Preparatory School (USMAPS) in Fort Monmouth, New Jersey instead of The University of Virginia. She attended USMAPS to prove to her family that a career in the military wasn't for her. Instead, it turned out to be the exact opposite. She loved it, thrived, and went to the United States Military Academy in West Point, New York the following year. Upon graduation, she was commissioned as an Army, Corps of Engineers officer. She married her college sweetheart, and

they have three children. She served in the Army within the US and internationally for 11 years, leading teams of various sizes in the Active, Reserves, and National Guard components. She was then hired as an Engineer with General Motors (GM) as a Supervisor in manufacturing. While at GM for 13 years in Michigan, she discovered that her career passion was more on the people side of the business (training, coaching, advising, guiding, developing, team building, etc.) in order to help teams and organizations operate more effectively. She went back for her Master of Training and Development with a focus on Organizational Development at Oakland University in Rochester, Michigan to equip and hone the skills needed for this path and has been excited to work in the Human Resources (HR) field for over 20 years. She returned to the DC/Maryland/Virginia area in 2008 to be close to family, and now works as an HR Leader with her company, where she continues to learn, grow, and prepare for higher leadership roles. She particularly has a heart for investing in young women and saw this book as an opportunity to apply her leadership and developmental experience and education to reach out to help more of them as they start to make choices in the beginning of their adult lives.

CPSIA information can be obtained
at www.ICGtesting.com
Printed in the USA
LVHW101321080621
PP16798300006BA/17